Charles Frederick Ball

About the Author

Brian Willan is a grandson of Alice Ball by her second marriage. A former publisher, he has written and edited a number of books in the field of South African history and holds honorary fellowships at several South African universities. He lives in Devon, England.

Charles Frederick Ball

*From Dublin's Botanic Gardens
to the Killing Fields of Gallipoli*

Brian Willan

The Liffey Press

Published by The Liffey Press Ltd
'Clareville', 307 Clontarf Road
Dublin D03 PO46, Ireland
www.theliffeypress.com

A catalogue record of this book is
available from the British Library.

ISBN 978-1-7397892-0-6

Printed in Ireland by SprintPrint.

Contents

This book is dedicated to the memory of
Eileen Ford, 1907-2003.

Preface

Charles Frederick Ball was one of the many young men whose life was cut short by the First World War. He was born and brought up in England, trained in horticulture at Kew but moved to Dublin in 1906 to take up a job at the Royal Botanic Gardens at Glasnevin. He was soon promoted to the position of Assistant Keeper, became the editor of *Irish Gardening*, and in a short space of time built up a reputation as one of Ireland's leading horticulturists. He was widely expected to succeed the Keeper, Sir Frederick Moore, when the time came for him to retire.

But then, in August 1914, war broke out. Ball enlisted in the Royal Dublin Fusiliers, was sent to Gallipoli and killed in action on 13 September 1915, one of thousands of casualties in a disastrous campaign. He was 35 years old.

C. F. Ball ('Fred' as he was known to friends and family) was my grandmother's first husband. Alice Lane was from an Anglo-Irish family and the two were married in Dublin in December 1914, just after he enlisted. I knew next to nothing about him. My mother mentioned his name a few times, as did my aunt Eileen, Alice's niece. I believe Eileen, when she was six or seven years old, had once met him.

I was not, I have to admit, all that interested.

That changed when I came across a small metal box containing over a hundred letters that Fred wrote to Alice between 1911 and 1914, along with a photograph album and several other items of memorabilia. Seven years after Fred died Alice married Robert Kinghan, my grandfather, and made a new life for herself in England, but she preserved these mementos, keeping them safe through various house moves. After Alice died in 1971 they passed to my mother. The first time I became aware of the metal box and its contents was after my mother died in 2018.

Intrigued by these letters, I set about finding out more about Fred's life and career, as well as his time with Alice. With the centenary of the First World War upon us it seemed a fitting time to do so. Further research I undertook elsewhere, in Ireland and England, has shed new light on Fred's brief but distinguished career as a horticulturist as well as his time as a soldier. This has encouraged me to write as rounded an account of his life as I can, and I have illustrated it with many of his own photographs – of both plants and people.

So what follows is Fred Ball's story – and, while the two of them were together, and for a while after, that of Alice too. I have done my best to do them justice.

Brian Willan
Uffculme, Devon, UK
March 2022

Foreword

Seamus O'Brien

One of my favourite destinations in London is the Royal Botanic Gardens, Kew, and, on entering the Victoria Gates, my first port of call will always be to the nearby Temple of Arethusa. Originally built as a folly for Princess Augusta's private botanic garden in 1758 by the celebrated architect Sir William Chambers, today it serves as a memorial for 'Kewites' who lost their lives in the two world wars. These visits have become a sort of pilgrimage to honour the memory of 'one of ours', Charles Frederick (Fred) Ball, who had previously worked at Kew as sub-foreman in the herbaceous and alpine department.

I say 'one of ours' because Fred (as he was known to his family and friends), a Leicestershire man, was later recruited by Sir Frederick Moore, Glasnevin's most famous Director, to the post of Assistant Keeper of what was then the Royal Botanic Gardens, Glasnevin. The gardens were at the pinnacle of their fame and were part of a trio of Royal Botanic Gardens located in Dublin, Edinburgh and at Kew in London. On a global scale they were the leading botanic gardens of their day and the greatest distribution centres of newly introduced plants during a time regarded as the golden era of plant exploration.

Charles Frederick Ball has been quite aptly described as one of the most gifted horticulturists of his generation. He moved to Glasnevin in December 1906 and was soon involved in the Garden's plant breeding programme involving the cross pollination of species of *Berberis*, *Calceolaria*, *Escallonia*, *Mahonia* and *Ribes*. Like other Glasnevin staff members he was a regular visitor to the Acton family's garden at Kilmacurragh in County Wicklow, now the National Botanic Gardens, Kilmacurragh, Glasnevin's country estate.

He was also actively involved in plant hunting expeditions to the mountains of Europe, befriending notable figures like King Ferdinand I of Bulgaria, a keen amateur botanist, and The O'Mahony of Kerry, Pierce O'Mahony, a noted plantsman and member of the old Irish (Gaelic) aristocracy. C. F. Ball's plant hunting exploits could be read at the time in *Irish Gardening*, a popular monthly of which he was editor.

Then, for an entire generation, the world changed with the outbreak of the Great War in 1914 and the gardens at Kew, Edinburgh and Glasnevin lost many of their finest and most experienced staff.

C. F. Ball decided to enlist in the famous 7th Battalion, Royal Dublin Fusiliers – the 'Pals'. Sent to Gallipoli, he managed to botanise between several fierce battles, writing of his finds to friends at Glasnevin and sending large consignments of seeds to Sir Frederick Moore. One was sent to Sir Frederick in August 1915 via another Glasnevin staff member, William Lacey, who had joined the Royal Irish Fusiliers and had also been sent to Gallipoli.

C. F. Ball's Gallipoli collections also reached another Irish friend, George Norman Smith, owner of the famous

Daisy Hill nursery near Newry in County Down. In 1937, as he prepared to retire from the nursery business, he offered Commander Frank Gilliland, who gardened at Brook Hall near Derry, an oak that had been raised from an acorn collected by 'a dear friend' and 'one of nature's gentlemen'. The oak in question was the Kermes oak, *Quercus coccifera*, a Mediterranean native, and had been raised by Smith decades previously from acorns gathered near the Gallipoli battlefields by C. F. Ball in 1915. Frank Gilliland planted the Gallipoli oak within view of the pond and flagstaff in the ancient walled garden at Brook Hall, and though the original has long-since vanished the current custodian, David Gilliland, plans to plant a replacement Kermes oak, thus perpetuating the memory of Charles Frederick Ball.

Ball was one of eleven men from the Royal Botanic Gardens, Glasnevin, who enlisted once war was declared. Of these, three left the gardens to fight and never returned. John Morgan was the first of Glasnevin's casualties. Originally from County Wicklow, Morgan was a member of the horticultural team and was killed in April 1915 in the incident famously known as Mouse Trap Farm, near Ypres in Belgium. Stephen Rose, an office worker and garden photographer, drowned aged just 25 in April 1917 when his ship was torpedoed by a U-boat in the Mediterranean Sea as it brought supplies to Egypt. However, it was the death of C. F. Ball on September 13 1915 that seemed to resonate most at Glasnevin and through the wider British and Irish horticultural communities. Following days of heavy shellfire, Ball was hit by a fragment mortally wounding him. One can only guess how Sir Frederick Moore and his staff reacted when the news reached Dublin. Fred Ball had thoroughly loved his work at Glasnevin and was passionate about plants. Shellfire and shrapnel had cut short what would have been an incredibly promising career at the age of just 35.

For Glasnevin it meant the loss of one of its most able and notable plantsmen. It is true to say that if the Great War had never happened, and if Charles Frederick Ball had not died at Gallipoli, he would undoubtedly have succeeded to the role of Keeper of the Royal Botanic Gardens when Sir Frederick Moore retired in April 1922.

In Dublin the tragic news first reached his widow, Alice, whom he had married in December 1914, shortly after he had enlisted in the Royal Dublin Fusiliers. Though she remarried in 1922, throughout her long life Alice preserved and treasured the many letters she received from her husband Fred, from 1911 until he left to go to war. These have proved to be an important reservoir for Brian Willan's biography of his grandmother's first husband.

C. F. Ball is remembered as one of Glasnevin's 'greats', and though his time there was cut short his name perseveres both there and at his earlier base, the Royal Botanic Gardens, Kew. Before he departed for the war Ball named one of his *Escallonia* hybrids for his bride, and to this day *Escallonia* 'Alice' takes pride of place in front of Glasnevin's Great Palm House, a living memorial to Alice and Fred.

After the war two further seedlings were named; *Escallonia* 'Glasnevin Hybrid' and *Escallonia* 'C. F. Ball'. The latter is undoubtedly the finest of this trio of seedlings, an evergreen shrub of two metres tall, bearing pendulous branches smothered in summer with blood-red flowers. In my opinion this is one of the finest cultivars ever raised at Glasnevin and it has received high praise over the years. It is absolutely apt that such an outstanding selection should bear the name of Glasnevin's famous Assistant Keeper.

Among the very first plants visitors meet on entering the gardens at Kilmacurragh, Glasnevin's rural annex in County Wicklow, are the three Glasnevin *escallonias*, with *Escallonia* 'Alice' and *Escallonia* 'C. F. Ball' flanking both sides of the entrance walk, thus ensuring their memory lives on.

A seedling of Kew's famous Verdun oak, planted at Kilmacurragh on November 11 2018 to mark the centenary of Armistice Day, commemorates Ireland's gardening war dead, including those from Kilmacurragh and Glasnevin; C. F. Ball and Kilmacurragh's Annesley Ball-Acton brothers come to mind when I pass it on a daily basis.

Fred Ball was just one of almost 49,400 men who left Ireland for the European battlefields and never returned. Sadly, all are buried in far-off lands, though they are remembered at the Irish National War Memorial Gardens near Dublin's Phoenix Park. Designed by Sir Edwin Lutyens, it was in that wonderful setting that a plant of *Escallonia* 'C. F. Ball' was planted in a dignified and moving occasion organised by the Irish Garden Plant Society in 2016. Thus *Escallonia* 'C. F. Ball' has come to symbolise the Great War in Irish horticulture, and this new and long awaited biography tells the story of one of Glasnevin's and Ireland's great horticultural heroes.

Seamus O'Brien
National Botanic Gardens of Ireland
Kilmacurragh, County Wicklow
March 2022

Acknowledgements

This book started with opening a box of old letters and led to me finding out a lot more about the man who wrote them than I imagined either likely or possible. This could not have happened without the help and support of many people and institutions I contacted along the way: I am grateful to all of them. In Ireland, the library and archives of the National Botanic Gardens, Glasnevin, have been an essential source of information about Fred Ball's time there between 1906 and 1914. At a time of Covid restrictions, and limited access to the library, Anna Teahan, the librarian and archivist, was my lifeline to its resources, and she went out of her way to help and to respond to my innumerable requests. This book would not have been possible otherwise. I owe thanks to individuals at a number of other institutions too: Rebecca McCormack and Meadhbh Murphy, Librarian and Deputy Librarian at the Irish Academy; Éilis Crowe, Archivist at the Guinness Archive in Dublin; Nora Thornton and Berni Metcalfe, National Library of Ireland; David Power, South Dublin Libraries, and the staff of the Clondalkin Library; Rebecca Hayes, Archivist and Curator, Grand Lodge of Freemasons of Ireland; Jonathan Maguire, Royal Irish Fusiliers Museum, Armagh.

In England, the archives of the Royal Botanic Gardens, Kew, have been a rich source of information about Fred Ball's time as a gardener between 1900 and 1903. Kat Harrington, Assistant Archivist and Julia Buckley, Illustrations Team, could not have been more helpful in retrieving relevant material for me, again through difficult Covid times. I am similarly grateful to John Weitzel, Loughborough Grammar School archivist, for passing on information from the school's records from Fred's time there in the 1890s, along with some splendid photographs; and to Liz Taylor, Royal Horticultural Society archivist, and her colleagues at the RHS Lindley Library, in relation to the E.A. Bowles papers.

The photographs in this book are a mixture of those I found in Fred and Alice's papers, or obtained from libraries and archives in England and Ireland, or from other private sources. I am grateful for permission to reproduce them in this book. My sincere thanks also to Lesley Fennell for permission to include in it the beautiful watercolour of *Escallonia* 'C.F. Ball' by her mother, Wendy Walsh.

One of the pleasures of a project like this has been the chance to meet others with a shared interest or connection to its subject. So my thanks to Jane Bolton, a granddaughter of Fred Ball's sister Connie, for passing on information about her family history, and for her kind hospitality when we met; David Gilliland for showing me around Brook Hall, just outside Derry in N. Ireland, where the 'Gallipoli oak' planted in Fred's memory once grew, and to David's father John Gilliland; Matt Holmes, Glasnevin Heritage, a mine of information on Glasnevin's history, for his interest in the project and for many kindnesses when I was in Dublin, and to James Mahon, for showing me around St Mobhi's church, Glasnevin; Tom Miniter, of the Dublin Naturalists'

Field Club, for his interest in Fred Ball, and for his generous hospitality when we met – and to Charles Shier, current Secretary of the Field Club; Carole Hope, for sharing the results of her research on Fred's friend and colleague Frank Laird, and Amy Abbott on the extended Kinghan family history; Seamus Shortall and Richard Page for information about Pierce O'Mahony, Richard's grandfather; Kathleen Maclure and Paul Nixon for delving into military and genealogical records on my behalf; Jim Clancy for help on preparing photographs; Roger Watts for memories of his grandfather, Hugh Anderson; Professor Roderick Floud for advice on the nature of gardening apprenticeships in the late nineteenth century; Dr E.C. Nelson, whose publications I have learnt much from, for additional advice and information; Margaret Carter and Mel Donnelly, Gallipoli Association and Commonwealth War Graves Commission respectively.

I am indebted to those who read earlier versions of the MS of this book. Their comments, corrections and suggestions have helped bring about a much improved end product. So thank you especially to Seamus O'Brien, to whom I am also indebted for writing the foreword for this book as well as taking the time to show me around the splendid gardens at Kilmacurragh in County Wicklow; and to Dr Martyn Rix, Professor Jeff Kildea, Carole Hope, Tom Miniter, Sean Connolly (of the Royal Dublin Fusiliers Association), and my wife Jenny, to whom I am grateful, as ever, for much else besides. All have generously contributed their time and expertise. I alone remain responsible, however, for the content of the final manuscript.

David Givens, of The Liffey Press, has been a brilliant publisher. I am grateful to him for taking this book on, knocking it into shape, producing it with a minimum of fuss, and then getting it out to the wider world.

Finally, this book is dedicated to the memory of Eileen Ford, my godmother, who died in 2003, aged 96. She remembered Fred Ball and she would have been interested in this book. I wish I had asked her more about him.

A Note on Names

Charles Frederick Ball never used his first name. As an adult, to the world beyond his family and closest friends, he was invariably 'C.F. Ball', and this is how he signed off his letters – preceded variously by 'Yours sincerely', 'Yours truly' or 'Yours faithfully', depending on his relationship with the recipient. Letters to him from colleagues in connection with his work, even those he knew well, would be addressed 'Dear Mr Ball', in keeping with the conventions of the time.

But within his family, and to his closest friends, he was 'Fred'. This is how he signed off the majority of his letters to Alice Lane, his fiancée, and later his wife. Occasionally, in his letters to her, there were variations, such as 'Frederick' and 'Freddie'. But he was never Charles.

In this book I have called him 'Fred' throughout. Sometimes this seems at odds with his public persona, represented by 'C.F. Ball', but in the interests of consistency this seemed the best thing to do. 'Fred' therefore encompasses both private and public personas.

Picture Sources and Credits

Alamy: 2, 42, 60 (bottom), 65 (bottom), 70; Author's private collection: 16 (top), 26, 28 (top), 43, 95; BBC N. Ireland: 115; Jane Bolton: 97; Sean Connolly: 150; Creative Commons: 18 (PD); 54 (CC BY-SA-2.5); 68 (bottom): (CC BY-SA-3.0); 69

29, 30, 31, 33 (x2); Royal Irish Academy © RIA: 79; Royal Irish Fusiliers Museum, Armagh, courtesy of Jonathan Maguire: 19; Seamus Shortall: 59; South Dublin Libraries: 106, 107 (x2), 156; *The Garden* (1899, 1909): 11 (top and middle), 52; *With Camera and Rücksack in the Oberland and Valais* (1913): 57; wwicemeteries.com, courtesy of Geerhard Joos and Terry Heard: 149.

The author and publisher gratefully acknowledge the permission granted to reproduce copyright material in this book. Every effort has been made to trace copyright holders and to obtain their permission for the use of copyright material. We would be pleased to rectify any errors or omissions in subsequent reprints or editions of this book.

Cover Photographs

Front cover (top): a view of the curvilinear range of glasshouses at the Botanic Gardens, Glasnevin, early 1900s, from the Laurence collection, National Library of Ireland; (middle): portrait of C.F. Ball in uniform taken by the Loughborough photographer, F. Newton Nield, early 1915 (Imperial War Museum); (bottom): watercolour (from a photograph) by Lt Drummond Fish of 'D' Company, Royal Dublin Fusiliers, in the trenches at Suvla Bay, Gallipoli, August 1915 (from *The Pals at Suvla Bay*, 1917).

Back cover: Coloured postcard, published by William Laurence, with a different view of the curvilinear range at the Botanic Gardens, Glasnevin, early 1900s.

Escallonia rubra 'C.F. Ball'.
Watercolour by Wendy Walsh.

I

Early Years

Fred Ball was born into a well-established local family in
Loughborough, a small market town in Leicestershire.
His father, Alfred, was a chemist and the family lived over
the shop at 14, High Street, in the middle of town. Alfred
Ball had taken over the business from his father in 1871 and
married Mary Bowley Kirby, from a nearby village, five
years later. He was 35, she 26. Mary was actually born in
Ohio in the United States where her parents had tried their
luck as farmers, but they had soon returned home.

Charles Frederick, 'Fred' to his family, was born on 13
October 1879. He was the third son, coming after Alfred
Kirby Ball (1877) and John Bramley Ball (1878). After Fred
there was a gap until Herbert in 1883, George Wilfred in
1884, and then a sister, Constance (Connie), in 1886.

The family were Methodists and Fred and his siblings
were baptized, so the church records show, in the nearby
Leicester Road Methodist church. As a seemingly prosperous
family, in a steady business, they had a live-in servant (Edith
Penny, aged 17, at the time of the 1881 census), as well as a
chemist's apprentice – Reuben Simmons, aged 16. When old
enough, the children would have gone to a nearby church
primary school. One of the boys, normally the eldest, would

The Market Place, Loughborough, as Fred Ball would have known it;
(below) the High Street, where the Ball family had their business and home.
Both photographs date from around 1900.

have been expected to join the family business and, in due course, to take it over.

Little is known of Fred's early years. He left only one childhood memory. A lady used to come to his home to give the children music lessons, he recalled, but he 'didn't like her at all and I'm afraid I took a dislike to the music lessons for that reason' – and ended up 'such an unmusical being and cannot even sing'.[1]

But in 1889, when Fred was nine, his father died, aged only 48. His death certificate records his occupation as 'retired chemist (pharmaceutical)', and states that he had suffered 'general paralysis' for three years before his death, probably the result of a stroke. It must have been an extraordinarily difficult time for the family. The business had to be sold and they moved to a new home – 86 Park Road, Loughborough, where Alfred died.[2]

A view of the main quad, Loughborough Grammar School, in 1895.

Classroom at Loughborough Grammar School, 1890s.

Mary, Fred's mother, was remembered as a talented artist. She is also recorded, in the 1891 census, as being 'partially deaf'. Descendants of Fred's sister Connie told me that later in life she used an ear trumpet.

Park Road, Loughborough, was close to the local grammar school, which could be one reason why they chose to move there. Fred became a pupil in February 1893, when he was 13. A note on the school register indicates that 'he fills his brother's place for this half term', and that 'he counts as a new boy next term'.[3] Quite what caused his elder brother John to leave mid-term is a mystery but it gave Fred his chance. Going to the grammar school at 13 was later than most, and it meant that he missed out on Latin which the younger boys took.

Loughborough Grammar School in the early 1890s had seen better days. Numbers were low and falling. The previous headmaster, John Colgrove, had recently left to set up a school of his own, taking some of the students with him, and inspectors' reports were critical. It had been years since any student from the school had gone on to one of the universities. Things started to improve, however, with the arrival of a new headmaster, Cecil Kaye, in 1893, the same year Fred joined the school.

Fred made a good start. In the examinations in the summer of 1894 his results were good enough to secure him an exhibition, relief for his mother from the school fees of £4 a year. He performed particularly well in French and Maths. By the Christmas term he was learning German too (third in the class), and came eighth out of eleven in the top set for maths. In the summer of 1895

Cecil Kaye, Headmaster, Loughborough Grammar School, between 1893 and 1900.

5

there was a similar spread of results: seventeenth in English, ninth in French, sixth in German, tenth (out of seventeen) in the top set for maths. Overall, he ended up twelfth out of nineteen. This might sound pretty average, but Fred was younger than his class mates, up to two years younger in some cases. In the light of this it was an impressive performance. Science, it should be noted, was not taught at all at this time.

Outside the classroom Fred would have welcomed the introduction of compulsory games in 1893, one of the changes made by Mr Kaye. Fred was a keen sportsman and good at cricket, football and tennis. A striking photo in the school archive shows that he was a member of the football team for the season 1894–95, despite being, as in class, younger and smaller than most of his teammates.

Staff and pupils, Loughborough Grammar School.
Cecil Kaye, the Headmaster, is standing in the middle.

The Loughborough Grammar School football team, 1894–95. Fred is standing, second from the left. Next to him are three teachers who also played in the team. Harry Linacre (sitting, second from left), went on to play for Nottingham Forest and England.

Fred left the Grammar School at the end of the summer term in 1895, aged 15. Despite the absence of any science teaching he had developed an interest in botany – it was his 'great delight' according to one report – and decided to apprentice himself to the firm of William Barron & Sons, landscape gardeners and nursery, in Elvaston, near Borrowash, in Derbyshire, 16 miles from Loughborough.[4] In April 1896, aged 16, he left home.

His indenture agreement has survived, preserved by Alice among her papers. Its language, and some of its terms, hark back to an earlier age. John Barron, owner of the firm, and son of the founder, undertook to teach him the 'Art of Nurseryman', and Fred agreed to be bound to him for a period of three years.

William Barron (1805–1891), founder of a famous nursery in Elvaston, Derbyshire, where Fred served his apprenticeship in the 1890s.

During this time he could not be married, he promised to 'respect and not to damage his property', he could not play cards, nor could he 'haunt Taverns or Playhouses nor absent himself from his Master's service unlawfully'. He was to be paid five shillings weekly for the first year, six shillings and six pence for the second year, and eight shillings for the third year. Fred's mother Mary had to sign the indenture agreement too since he was under 21, and had to pay John Barron a premium, or deposit, of £25.⁵

Accommodation was not covered in the agreement, so Fred must have had to find digs nearby and pay for this from his modest weekly salary, returning home – as he recalled many years later – at weekends. Compared to most other gardening apprentices embarking upon their training he was both older and a lot better educated.[6]

William Barron & Sons was a successful and well established company. They combined landscape gardening for the landed gentry with the supply of seeds and plants of all kinds to a growing market of domestic gardeners. The firm had been started by William Barron, originally from Scotland, who came south to work for Charles Stanhope, 4th Earl of Harrington, at Elvaston Castle. He transformed what had been a largely featureless site into one of the most celebrated gardens in Europe, open to the public from the 1850s. He went on to gain a reputation as one of the country's leading landscape gardeners, and was famous for his expertise in transplanting trees, inventing an ingenious machine to help carry out these often very difficult operations.[7]

Elvaston Castle gardens in the 1870s.

William Barron's famous tree transplanting machine.

William Barron died a few years before Fred began his apprenticeship, and the business was run by his son John. Trees (especially conifers) and shrubs remained a speciality, but as an apprentice Fred, so he recalled later, 'worked through every department of the nursery', and gained plenty of experience working in glasshouses. Keen to get on, and to develop his artistic skills, he also took some evening classes, attending the Ockwood and Borrowash Art Classes nearby. He gained a first-class certificate in Elementary Drawing (Freehand) and a second-class certificate in Elementary Drawing (Perspective).[8] His grammar school education, even if only of two years' duration, must have given him a good head start.

Fred remained with William Barron & Sons for six months after the completion of his apprenticeship. John

Barron must have been sad to lose him. 'We have always found him very industrious and attentive to his duties, and anxious to learn,' he wrote in a testimonial, and he wished him well in his desire to 'better himself' elsewhere.[9]

Fred's next job took him south: to the firm of Peter Barr & Sons in Long Ditton, near Surbiton, Surrey. Their speciality was not trees and shrubs but flowers which they cultivated, imported and sold in vast quantities. Peter Barr, the founder of the firm, was one of the great nineteenth century horticulturists, and still on the scene – albeit away on a lengthy world tour – when Fred joined the company in May 1899.[10] His particular enthusiasm was daffodils and he was widely known as the 'daffodil king', his nursery considered 'the most famous daffodil grounds in the world'.[11] Their catalogue boasted over 600 varieties of daffodil and they had won innumerable medals. His nursery had become a tourist attraction in its own right and people used to take the train from London to see his spectacular displays.

'A visit to the famous nurseries at Surbiton at almost any season of the year', so the *Gardeners' Chronicle*

Peter Barr, the 'daffodil king'; Peter Rudolph, one of the three sons who took over the business; and the cover of one of Barr & Sons' catalogues, 1900.

thought, 'is of the greatest interest to the horticulturist, and those who seek for new things, especially in the time of the daffodil and tulip,' and was matched 'by few other nurseries in the world'.

Peter Barr's three sons – Rudolph, William and George – now ran the business, carrying it on much as before. Rudolph, the eldest, shared his father's enthusiasm for daffodils and raised many new hybrids.[12] But they grew and sold much else besides, including 'irises, peonies, sunflowers, michaelmas daisies, and other hardy herbaceous, alpine and bulbous plants', and at Long Ditton there were 'substantial rock and aquatic gardens' too.[13]

But after a year in the Herbaceous Department at Peter Barr & Sons Fred moved on, keen to improve himself and his prospects. The Royal Botanic Gardens, Kew, the world's leading botanic and horticultural institution, was the place to do this, and it was no more than a few miles down the road from where he lived and worked. Maybe this was already in his mind when he took the job at Barr & Sons. Experience and qualifications from Kew, he would have been well aware, were a passport to the best jobs in horticulture, and the accepted route for any ambitious young man to make his way in the profession.

So in May 1900 Fred wrote off to apply. 'I should very much like to enter Kew to gain further knowledge in the gardening line,' he said, adding that he had been 'trying to prepare myself for some time.'[14] He completed the necessary application form, supplied testimonials from his current and former employers, and said that he believed he met all their requirements, being 'the required age (between 20 and 25)', 'free from physical defect and above average height', and had had good experience under glass at Messrs Barron & Son.[15]

When he was accepted he wrote back to ask if they could 'recommend a good book on wild flowers and their habitats' (which gave an indication of his interests) as he wanted to 'prepare myself so as to make the best of my time while on your staff'.[16] Maybe it was this, assuming Kew responded to his request, that helped Fred to identify the *Mentha arvensis* hybrid which he found some weeks later on the edge of Richmond Park, close to where he lived.[17]

Fred's weekly pay at Kew was to be no more than 21 shillings a week, probably less than he had been getting with Barr & Sons. But nobody went to Kew for the money: it was the training and the prestige that counted, and you were expected to consider it a privilege to be there. Kew liked to call itself the 'University of Horticulture'. Money would have to wait.

Working in the Temperate House, Kew, c. 1900.

2

Training at Kew

Fred Ball arrived at Kew as a gardener in July 1900, three months before his 21st birthday. Kew Gardens was at the height of its prestige, at the centre of the empire as well as the world of plants. It employed 150 people, 60 of them gardeners. It ran an estate that extended over 300 acres, had numerous glasshouses, three museums, an extensive library and a herbarium, and looked after tens of thousands of plants, trees and shrubs. Under the autocratic guidance of its Director, Sir William Thistleton-Dyer, Kew presided over, and added to, the largest collection of living plant species in the world, its activities increasingly addressed to the economic needs of empire. Commercially valuable plants – producing commodities like quinine, rubber or cotton – were introduced from one part of the empire to another, studied, propagated and improved at Kew along the way. Every year over 10,000 specimens, in one form or another, were distributed to over 130 botanical institutions. Many lives, across the world, were transformed as a consequence.[1]

Postcard of the exterior of the Temperate House, 1902, where Fred began his career at Kew. (below): Inside the central block of the Temperate House, 1900. The tall palm is Rhapis excelsa *(bamboo palm), from China.*

But Victorian Kew Gardens was also a provider of leisure and entertainment. Around one and a half a million visitors came each year to see the trees and plants on display, making demands, for example, for a tea room, that were often not welcomed by Sir William and his staff. There was always a tension between scientific purpose and public access.

Fred worked initially in the Temperate House. This was the largest Victorian glasshouse in the world, covering well over an acre, and was finally completed the year before Fred arrived at Kew. Its purpose was to provide the conditions for plants from temperate regions to flourish and to protect them from frost. A new heating system had transformed growing conditions, many species taking on a new life, and the existing collections of plants were rearranged by geographical region, each allocated to a separate part of the building and kept at a different temperature. It worked well and the Temperate House was a popular attraction for visitors, particularly the 'Himalayan House' (the northern wing) which had an extensive collection of Rhododendrons as well as other plants from China and Japan.[2] The central block, known often as the 'Winter Garden', was filled with plants from Australasia, while the 'Mexican House' (the southern wing) was devoted to cactuses and other succulents.

The 'Mexican House', the southern wing of the Temperate House, home to cactuses and other succulents.

Lonicera hildebrandiana
and Rosa gigantea, *two of*
the most striking plants in
the Temperate House.

Fred was one of eight gardeners who looked after the plants in the Temperate House. They were supervised by the foreman, William Dallimore, and spent most of their time cleaning, watering, potting and propagating. They were also expected to deal with questions from visitors – and to be on the lookout for the less scrupulous among them who tried to make off with cuttings.[3]

Other visitors came with more reputable intent. Two that William Dallimore particularly remembered were General Sir Henry Collett and Sir Dietrich Brandis, in their sixties and seventies respectively, old India hands who had developed a serious interest in botany and were now busy writing books. Both men were 'greatly interested' in the *Lonicera hildebrandiana* and *Rosa gigantea*, which were growing in the Himalayan House. When the former (a giant Burmese honeysuckle that could grow to 12 metres high) began to flower, Dallimore recalled, he fixed a ladder to the rafters so the two men could make a close inspection of the blossoms when they came on their daily visits.[4] It must have made the staff a bit nervous.

Another distinguished visitor at this time – and somebody whose path would cross with Fred's a decade later – was Dr Augustine Henry, the well known sinologist and plant collector. He had introduced into western Europe hundreds of hitherto unknown species from China, where he had worked for years for the Imperial Customs Service. Now, in 1901 and 1902, he was back in England and spending a lot of his time at Kew, writing up his most recent discoveries.

Lilium henryii, *named after Dr Augustine Henry.*

On one occasion, Dallimore remembered, Dr Henry came to the Temperate House and was particularly struck by their *Lilium henryii*, named after him, which he had brought into cultivation in England. A beautiful lily with deep orange flowers, it had flourished in the benign conditions of the Himalayan House at Kew and had grown a strong stem with over 50 flowers in the head. In its wild state in China, Dr Henry said, he had never seen a stem with more than seven flowers, and usually it had less than five. That must have been quite satisfying to hear if it was your job to look after it.[5]

Gardeners at Kew did not have it easy. For most of the year their working day lasted from 6.00 am to 6.00 pm, Mondays to Saturday, and they were expected, at the insistence of Sir William Thiselton-Dyer, to report for duty in blue serge suits and dark grey flannel shirts with turned-down collars ('for the sake of appearances and also in the

Sir William Thiselton-Dyer, Director of the Royal Botanic Gardens, Kew, 1885–1904.

interests of the men's health'). The salary – gardeners were paid little more than the labourers at Kew – was barely enough to live on and was a frequent cause for complaint.

Dallimore's view was that the authorities were more inclined to point out 'how much the young men gained from the privilege of being allowed to work at Kew' than to remember 'what the young men were doing for Kew'. Sometimes they were required to work on Sundays, but at least they got paid extra for that.[6]

Senior staff at Kew, 1902. Fred worked under William Dallimore, foreman in the Temperate House (last on right); Charles Raffill (sitting, second from left), who succeeded Dallimore in 1901; and Walter Irving (first on left), foreman in the Herbaceous and Alpine Department.

*Dr J.G. Baker, formerly Keeper of the Herbarium and Library at Kew,
lecturing to young gardeners on Systematic Biology in 1903.*

Kew did offer opportunities for Fred and his fellow
gardeners. Lectures were put on for those keen to learn more
but they usually took place after normal working hours,
were often poorly attended and the authorities refused
requests to make them part of the working day. Moreover,
the content of the lectures was hopelessly out of date, and
many of the gardeners considered them too theoretical.
Even the Director thought they were not of much use. He
valued practical instruction and experience far more highly,
and did nothing to bring them up to date. Fred, though,
was keen to know more about the science of botany, not
just practical horticulture, and this did not put him off. He
was duly awarded certificates in 1900 and 1901 for having
attended lectures in British Botany, Elementary Physics
and Chemistry, Geographical Botany, and Organography
and Systematic Botany. His lecturer for the last-named was
Dr J.G. Baker, recently retired from his position as Keeper

Staff at Kew, 1903. Fred is standing in the third row, last but one on left.

of the Herbarium and Library and memorably described by Beatrix Potter, who had met him a couple of years earlier, as 'a slim, timid-looking old gentleman' with 'an appearance of having been dried in blotting paper under a press'. Further qualifications, including a certificate in Advanced Botany, came Fred's way as a result of attending evening classes at a college in South Kensington.[7]

In addition to these formal lectures a programme of more informal talks and discussion was organised by the Kew Gardens Mutual Improvement Society, of which Fred was – in 1902–03 – joint secretary. The programme he organised, so it was reported, 'proved to be one of the most successful of recent years', and he was an enthusiastic participant. Fred was commended, along with his friend Eric Brown, for having attended all 22 meetings, and his paper on 'Hardy Conifers' was winner that year of the prestigious Hooker prize, named after Sir Joseph Hooker,

Kew's famous director. Both Fred and another prize-winner, John W. Campbell – an Irishman from Killarney, County Kerry – were also complimented for their contribution to discussions.[8] The Mutual Improvement Society, it is clear,

The Royal Botanic Gardens, Kew, as it was in the first decade of the twentieth century.

was an important training ground for these young gardeners. According to William Dallimore, recalling their meetings later in life, everyone agreed that it was 'an excellent institution', and 'many a young fellow, who was tongue-tied during his early attendances, learned to express himself before an audience'.[9]

The Kew cricketers, Fred among them, were to be commended too. 'Thanks to the kindly interest of the Director and Curator the club now possess an excellent pitch for practice,' and they had a new pavilion too. That season, 1902–03, they won 5, lost 3 and drew 1. The highlight was an away victory over Chiswick House, whose team included two county cricketers. 'The failure of their best bats,' it was reported, 'was due to some wonderful bowling by Mr Ball.'[10]

Front page of the menu for the 1905 Kew Guild dinner.

Gardeners at Kew were also encouraged to join the Kew Guild. This provided a social forum for those who worked there, and it aimed to foster a sense of camaraderie between 'Kewites' as they went out into the wider world. Each year they had an annual dinner, open to past and present Kewites, several of which Fred attended while he was at Kew – and continued to do so after he had left. In May 1903, for example, he and his fellow Kewites dined at the Holborn Restaurant in London and listened to a typically self-congratulatory after-dinner speech from Sir William Thistelton-

Annual dinner of the Kew Guild, held at the Holborn Restaurant, London, 29 May 1905. Fred is seated on the far side of the second table from the front. One of the guests of honour that evening was Dr Augustine Henry, the eminent botanist, plant collector and sinologist.

Dyer, reminding everybody present of the benefits that Kew bestowed. 'It was good for the young countryman at Kew at a critical period of his life when character was being formed and friendships started to be helped to find confidence in himself and trust in others,' he said. 'It was equally good for him later in his career to be kept in touch with his early associates and friends, to learn of them and their work and to feel that they were interested in his efforts too.'[11]

But there was some substance to what he said. Many Kewites did form strong bonds and friendships that could last a lifetime. Fred was affable and by all accounts made friends easily, but we know he developed a particular friendship with Eric Brown, who went on to make a career for himself in Uganda. John Besant, a Scotsman, who arrived at Kew in 1901, and worked in the Tropical Fern House and then the Succulent House, was another he got to know well. Later they would become colleagues in Glasnevin. 'Although we did not work in the same Department,' Besant recalled, 'I was often associated with him on the cricket field, and in botanical rambles no one was more generally liked at Kew than Ball.' For a while Fred was secretary of the British Botanical Club at Kew so may well have been the organiser of these 'botanical rambles'.[12]

After nearly two years at Kew, his abilities recognised, Fred was promoted to the position of sub-foreman in the Herbaceous and Alpine Department, and his salary increased from 21 to 27 shillings a week. Here he came under Walter Irving, described as 'a man of a very modest, retiring disposition' but always willing to place his 'extensive knowledge' at the service of others. Like Fred he had come

The rock garden at Kew, opened to the public in 1882.
It quickly became one of the principal attractions.

to Kew as a student gardener but he never left. He had been foreman in charge of the department since 1893 and had built up a reputation as an authority on alpine plants.[13] Irving was soon impressed with his new sub-foreman, considering him to be 'exceptionally clever and capable'.[14]

The rock garden seems to have become Fred's responsibility as sub-foreman. It was a relatively recent addition to the displays at Kew, constructed from scratch in 1882 in order to accommodate some three thousand alpine plants, a gift from the estate of George Curling Joad, a botanist and plant collector. The winding path laid down between rocks on either side aimed to represent the course of a typical Pyrenean stream, and it proved highly popular with visitors. Over the years many new plants and species were added. *Saxifraga*, according to Walter Irving, were the most

THE ROCKERY.
KEW GARDENS.

Another view of the rock garden from a postcard sent on 5 September 1905. It shows a member of the Royal Botanic Gardens Constabulary keeping an eye on things.

The dripping well, part of the rock garden.

numerous genus in the rock garden, and by Fred's time there were some 200 species and varieties. Half-way along the rock garden there was a dripping well for plants that thrived on moisture, while a small unheated greenhouse – the Alpine House – housed plants that bloomed in winter and early spring and needed some protection from the cold and wet.[15]

Alpine plants would become one of Fred's passions, although he preferred to see them in their native habitat, and he would later embark upon several plant-collecting expeditions in the mountains of Europe. The year he spent as sub-foreman in the Herbaceous and Alpine Department at Kew must have left its mark.

* * *

Fred left Kew in August 1903. He had taken full advantage of what it had to offer and had gained valuable experience. Gardeners were not expected to stay for longer than three years, and most then went on to positions as head gardeners or foremen on landed estates, or to jobs in commercial nurseries or the colonial service overseas – the destination of both Eric Brown and John Campbell.[16]

As one of the best qualified of his contemporaries Fred would not have been short of offers if he had wished to go down one of these routes. However, he decided instead to set up a market garden and nursery business with his younger brother, Wilfred, in Keyworth, Nottinghamshire. Unfortunately, the venture did not work out well. They persevered for three years but in the end they fell out. On 25 July 1906, it was announced that the partnership of 'Charles Frederick Ball and George Wilfred Ball, market gardeners at Keyworth, under the style of Ball Bothers', was dissolved, and Fred sold his share of the business.[17]

In need of employment, Fred then wrote to Kew to see if they might have a job for him. William Watson, the Curator, replied that the only vacancy they had was for a gardener. Fred decided to take it. Although this was inferior to the position of sub-foreman he had before, he told Watson he would accept his offer, and hoped he might be able to rejoin Walter Irving in the Herbaceous and Alpine Department. He returned to Kew on 30 July 1906. Most likely there was a promise of promotion to sub-foreman as soon as such a position became vacant.[18]

In the event he did not have long to wait, and a few weeks later, on 17 September, he was promoted to sub-foreman, effectively the same job he had left three years before. Watson thought Fred 'a much better man than one or two of

The water lily pond at Kew, c. 1900.

our foremen' and was ready to promote him further should a vacancy arise. Otherwise it was inevitable that he would leave for a better position elsewhere.

It is clear, from a splendid team photo, that Fred arrived in time to take some part in the cricket season, and it was a chance to renew old acquaintances at Kew as well as to make some new ones. One friendship that dated from this time was with Herbert Cowley who was working in the Orchid Department, having come to Kew after a spell at Veitch's, one of England's leading nurseries. After Kew, Cowley moved into gardening journalism and it would not be long before he was encouraging Fred to contribute to the journals he worked for. Later they would go off on plant-collecting expeditions together.

Fred's second spell at Kew lasted no more than a few months. His next move came about when Frederick Moore, Keeper of the Royal Botanic Gardens at Glasnevin, Dublin, found himself in need of a new outdoor foreman.

The position was occupied by William Parnell who was 73 years old and had been in the job for nearly 40 years. But in September 1906 Parnell had to stop work, suffering from cancer, and it was obvious that he would not be returning. This left Moore exposed, for there was nobody at Glasnevin capable of taking his place, and he soon found it impossible, in Parnell's absence, to manage the day-to-day work of the labourers, many of them illiterate, who kept the Gardens functioning.

So he wrote to his friend William Watson at Kew to ask if he could recommend somebody suitable. Watson replied that he thought Frederick Ball was his man. He was 'an excellent fellow in every way, gentlemanly, quiet, good looking, age 27, height 5 ft 10 in., rings true however tried,

Herbert Cowley was at Kew during Fred's second spell there. He left to join the staff of The Garden *and would later accompany Fred on a plant-collecting trip to Bulgaria.*

The past and present Kewites cricket match which took place during Fred's time at Kew in 1906. He is standing in the third row, last but one on the left.

and loyal. Professionally he has had the sort of training your place requires,' and he was now 'waiting for a suitable appointment at home or abroad.' He offered to release Fred to visit Dublin if Moore wished to see him.[19]

The day after Moore received Watson's letter recommending Fred he received another letter from Arthur Bulley, who ran Bees Nursery in Chester, suggesting an alternative: John Besant, Fred's contemporary at Kew, who he employed as an assistant manager in his nursery. Unsure about which of the two to go for, Moore wrote again to William Watson, who knew both men well, but he declined to express a preference.[20]

*The Palm House at Kew and the
formal gardens (below) which surrounded it.*

William Parnell died at the end of November, but an obstacle to his replacement then arose. The Department of Agriculture and Technical Instruction in Dublin, which had to approve any new appointment at this level, wanted an Irish candidate and found it difficult to believe that one could not be found. Appointments to the civil service were a sensitive matter, particularly at a time when Ireland was edging towards home rule, and the Department anticipated political scrutiny. Moore was adamant, however, that he needed not just 'a man with a good horticultural training', who could be found locally, but a 'man with a thorough technical training and knowledge of botanic garden work . . . well up in the British flora, and who has an all round knowledge of outdoor plants, herbaceous plants, alpine plants, trees and shrubs.'

'To have such a knowledge,' Moore argued, 'a man must have been trained in a botanic garden.'[21] He explained why no such person existed in Ireland, and in the end the Department relented. Moore chose Fred over Besant and on 10 December 1906 he arrived in Dublin for a trial period.

'It will be a great relief to have someone in charge,' Moore told the Department the next day. 'It has been very hard to keep things going.'[22] A month later, in January 1907, Fred's temporary appointment as outdoor foreman was made permanent.

3

Assistant Keeper, Royal Botanic Gardens, Glasnevin

In the first decade of the twentieth century the Royal Botanic Gardens enjoyed an enviable reputation. One of a network of botanical gardens spread out across the empire, it had a longer history and deeper roots than most. Ireland's gardens had its origins in the late eighteenth century, established by the Dublin Society and funded by the Irish parliament. In 1906 Ireland no longer had a parliament of its own but the Botanic Gardens remained an admired national institution, comparable to the best in the world, and visited by over 400,000 people each year. Like its counterparts elsewhere, it combined research and instruction with the preservation and breeding of plants, shrubs and trees from Ireland and overseas.

The Gardens spread out over 50 acres in Glasnevin, not far from the centre of Dublin. It had a spectacular curvilinear range of glasshouses, designed by the famous Dublin-born iron founder and manufacturer, Richard Turner, as well as an impressive glass palm house, both of them dating from the mid-nineteenth century. Turner had constructed the Palm House at Kew, and had a hand in the Temperate House, so what Fred found at Glasnevin must have felt familiar.

Portrait of Fred Ball by his brother Herbert,
a professional photographer, c. 1904.

Glasnevin's collection of carnivorous plants, orchids and cacti were the most popular attractions. Seeds and plants to keep the whole enterprise going were acquired from commercial nurseries, by donation, and through exchange with other botanical gardens and individual gardeners. Maintaining and nurturing these relationships was essential to its successful operation.

Frederick Moore, the Keeper, had been in the post since 1879, having succeeded his father David. He was considered a practical horticulturist rather than a botanist, a gardener not a scientist, but he was held in high regard and during his time the Royal Botanic Gardens both flourished and expanded. Orchids were his passion, so it is no surprise that Glasnevin should have built up an extensive collection, one of the finest in the world. Several species indeed would be named after both Moore and his wife Phylis, whom he had married in 1901. *Nerine* and *Lachenalia*, South African genera, were among Moore's other enthusiasms, and he had embarked upon an intensive breeding programme.[1]

Sir Frederick Moore, Keeper of the Royal Botanic Gardens, 1879–1922, at around the time Fred first met him; Rosamund Pollock, one time 'lady gardener' and later Moore's secretary and 'technical assistant'.

Other senior staff at Glasnevin had been there for just as long. Apart from Parnell, the outside foreman, whose death had led to Fred's appointment, Frederick Moore relied on David McArdle, whose father had worked at Glasnevin before him. He had begun as plant collector and clerk and was now in charge of seed exchange and the library. Paddy Pope had likewise been there for years, as had his father before him, and he occupied the position of indoor foreman when Fred arrived to become the outdoor equivalent in 1906.

*Two views of the curvilinear range of glasshouses at the
Botanic Gardens, Glasnevin, early twentieth century.*

The Great Palm House at Glasnevin, early twentieth century,
one of the Botanic Gardens' main attractions.

Rosamund Pollock had only arrived in 1902 but she played as important a part as anybody in keeping things going. She started as a 'lady gardener' but by 1904 she had become secretary to Frederick Moore and proved to be highly proficient at typing and shorthand. She combined this secretarial role with being his 'technical assistant', which involved taking charge of the plant books, catalogues and the supervision of seed collection. Moore would have found it difficult to function without her.[2]

Fred's trial period could hardly have gone better. 'I beg to report that he has given unqualified satisfaction,' Moore told the assistant secretary at the Department of Agriculture and Technical Instruction. 'He has readily fallen into the ways of the place. He has organised his men well, and he has got on with them without any friction whatever. In fact, as far as I can indirectly ascertain, they all like him.'[3] In short, Fred had

Portrait of Fred Ball, c. 1910.

proved to be, Moore informed Colonel David Prain, the new Director at Kew, 'a great success'.[4]

Checking plant names and labels was one of Fred's first tasks. 'My new foreman Ball is backing me up well in my efforts to get things right, and to get our names as correct as possible,' Moore was pleased to say in March 1907, adding that he intended to 'push it on as far as I can'. Crocuses, it seems, were one of the problem areas. Fortunately, Moore was on friendly terms with E.A. Bowles, an English horticulturist who knew more about this genus than anybody alive, and he offered to help too. In reply, Moore thanked him and told him to expect some more detailed queries from Fred to follow shortly.[4]

So impressed was Moore with his new outside foreman that he decided to seek authorisation to appoint an Assistant Keeper. In making his case he pointed out that hitherto he had to do all the scientific work, plant labelling, herbaceous work, and correspondence, and he was in urgent need of somebody to share the burden. He wanted Fred in this new role but he still had an eye on John Besant, who he had liked too, as a replacement for Fred in the outdoor foreman job should his plans for the new position be approved.[5]

Things duly fell into place. Fred was appointed Assistant Keeper, on a salary of £110 per annum, although only after he had taken and passed the civil service examination in June 1907, and John Besant arrived at Glasnevin as outdoor foreman on 1 July. Again the issue of the lack of suitable local candidates for the position of assistant keeper came up. And nearly two years later, when a question was raised in the House of Commons by Patrick O'Shaughnessy, an Irish Nationalist MP, it had to be explained that 'there were no men in the Department's service with the special qualifications and experience required for the post.'[6]

So Fred stepped into a much bigger job, taking over many of the responsibilities which Moore had hitherto shouldered alone. These included, Moore elaborated, 'supervising the naming and labelling of plants, identifying specimens, making catalogues of plants, keeping plant books, answering technical correspondence, collecting and drying specimens for a reference herbarium, and other like duties'.[7] To this might be added the task of hosting distinguished visitors and delegations when Moore was away, a not infrequent requirement. There would be plenty, it was clear, to keep him busy. Fred's appointment enabled Moore to embark upon several extended overseas trips, and to spend more of his time advising the government on wider educational and horticultural matters, secure in the knowledge that the affairs of the Gardens were in capable hands while he was away or otherwise engaged.

Fred slotted in easily and his new job brought him into contact with everyone who worked there. Already a popular figure, people found him quiet and unassuming, but enthusiastic about his work and knowledgeable about all kinds of plants, practically as well as scientifically. Frederick Moore's view was that he fulfilled his duties 'with credit and success'.[8]

The relationship between Fred and John Besant could have been awkward but they seem to have got on perfectly well. They shared an interest in alpine plants and they would sometimes travel together, for example on visits to commercial nurseries. A couple of years later Fred would remark that he was fortunate to be working with so agreeable a colleague. Others, it has to be said, considered Besant somewhat dour but Fred thought he was 'a real decent sort'.[9] Together they brought new professionalism and expertise to the running of the Gardens.

Fred was particularly interested in plant-breeding and Glasnevin provided the opportunity to pursue this. He took over the breeding programme for *Nerine* and *Lachenalia*, continuing the work initiated by Frederick Moore, and he embarked upon the production of new garden varieties of *Calceolaria*, *Escallonia*, *Berberis* and *Mahonia*, as well as *Ribes* and *Campanula*.[10] Later on he created a *Saxifraga* hybrid, the result of successfully crossing *S.umbrosa* with *S.* × *geum*

'Not difficult to cross', Fred said of Lobelia *'Morning Glow' (left) in 1908. (right) A present-day* Saxifraga×geum/ Saxifraga umbrosa *hybrid.*

*A stroll in the Botanic Gardens: postcard of the bridge and lake
at Glasnevin, early twentieth century.*

(*S.hirsuta*), which he would exhibit in 1912. This may well
be the plant that acquired the name *Saxifraga* 'C.F. Ball',
recorded as being distributed from Glasnevin a decade later.[11]

Fred soon showed his worth as an ambassador for the
work of the Royal Botanic Gardens, always an important
consideration given its dependence upon public funding. He
would often be asked to be a judge at horticultural shows
in and around Dublin – such as the Trim show in August
1908 – or to give lectures to meetings of the Irish Gardeners'
Association or other local societies. In November 1907, for
example, he delivered a lecture to the St Andrews Guild,
Bray, on the subject of 'Insectivorous Plants.'[12] He already
had an ability to turn his hand to just about any horticultural
subject.

Fred also began, from late 1907, to contribute to the
gardening journals, including *The Garden* (his friend Herbert
Cowley was now on its staff) and the *Gardeners' Chronicle*,
the leading periodical of the day. He would often write about

Fred's photo of orchids in bloom in the orchid house, October 1909.

particular plants at Glasnevin, such as *Verbascum leianthum*, of which they had several. The largest stood 14 feet high: it had 'a bold and imposing appearance, and is planted in front of a row of evergreen shrubs, which form a fine background, so that the towering spike of yellow blossoms attracts attention from a considerable distance.'[13]

Irish Gardening, which began in 1906, published his articles too. The first was on 'Water Gardening' in September 1907, and others soon followed: on *Coelogyne mooreana*, a white orchid from Vietnam, named after Frederick Moore; *Sophora tetraptera*, a fruit-bearing tree from New Zealand which had thrived in the Irish climate and had grown to 26 feet; and *Spiraea ariaefolia (Holodiscus discolor)*, which he recommended to anyone 'requiring a really hardy, free flowering shrub to produce white flowers in July'.[14] Often Fred's articles were illustrated by his own photographs, reproduced in black

Thomas and George Smith, proprietors of the
Daisy Hill Nursery, Newry.

and white, which he developed himself. He covered a wide range of plants, supplied accurate descriptions of their characteristics, information about how they came to be at Glasnevin, what had to be done to enable them to thrive. He had an easy writing style, avoiding excessive technical or taxonomic detail, and acute powers of observation. Many readers, Fred would have hoped, would be inspired to come and see the real thing.

Fred's work often took him outside Dublin. Armed, at the beginning, with introductions from Frederick Moore – Sir Frederick as he became in 1911 – he would visit commercial nurseries to buy or exchange seeds or plants. With the owners of several of these he developed close working relationships and friendships – the Donard nursery in Newcastle, County Down, McGredy's in Portadown, Dicksons, which had

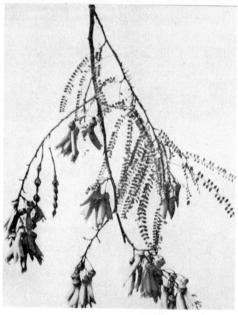

Grindelia integrifolia (top), *an example
of which was obtained from Canada by the
Daisy Hill nursery and sent to Kew for
identification; (below) Fred's photograph
of* Sophora tetraptera, *from New
Zealand, 'flowering unusually well'
at Glasnevin, May 1909.*

several branches in both the north and south.[15] Foremost among them, though, were Thomas and George Smith, father and son, proprietors of the Daisy Hill Nursery in Newry. It was considered to be one of Europe's leading commercial nurseries, stocked with an enormous range of seeds and plants from all parts of the world, and it had a relationship with Glasnevin that went back to the 1880s. Fred worked closely with both of them and once commented that 'Mr T. Smith is not slow to recognise a good plant.'[16] George Smith shared the experience with Fred of having worked for Peter Barr's nursery in England (though not quite at the same time). He later described Fred as 'a dear friend'.[17]

On occasion Fred obtained seeds and plants from the Daisy Hill

Fred's photo of a six feet high Cordyline indivisa *'Vera',*
taken during a visit to the Walpole family's garden at
Mount Usher, County Wicklow.

Nursery which nobody at Glasnevin was able to identify, for example a variety of *Grindelia* which Thomas Smith said came from Vancouver Island in Canada. The solution, when this kind of difficulty arose, was to consult Kew, the source of wisdom on such matters – over the years Frederick Moore had sent them dozens of similar enquiries. Fred's former colleagues rarely failed him, successfully identifying this specimen as *Grindelia integrifolia* (Puget Sound gumweed).

Another time, in 1911, neither Mr Smith nor Fred were able to identify an 'interesting' fungus that had attacked his *Abelia*. Again Kew came up with the answer.[18]

In fact Fred corresponded regularly with Kew throughout his time at Glasnevin, visiting them whenever he got the opportunity. He sent specimens for identification from a variety of other sources too. Among them were plants he had collected himself in Switzerland and Bulgaria. Once, in 1913, a specimen of *Deutzia* (Vilmorin 4277), a deciduous shrub from China, which Fred sent to William Bean, the Assistant Curator in charge of the Arboretum, matched nothing they could find and it was declared a new species. That summer it flowered at both Kew and Glasnevin, the first time it had done so.[19]

Ashbourne House, Glounthaune, County Cork,
residence and fine garden of Richard Beamish.

An autochrome lumière colour photograph of the herbaceous border at the Botanic Gardens, dating from 1910 or 1911. Fred wrote about the herbaceous border in Irish Gardening *in December 1911 and may well have taken this photograph.*

As well as dealing with commercial nurseries in Ireland, Fred was a regular visitor to the owners and head gardeners of the country's great landed estates, still in their prime. The exchange of seeds and plants was central to these interactions too, and Sir Frederick Moore, and his father before him, had made a point of offering plants to the owners of these estates and other leading gardeners if considerations of soil or climate meant they were more likely to flourish elsewhere. Since Moore considered the climate at Glasnevin 'fairly harsh' and the soil 'poor', there was good reason to do so.[20]

One beneficial side effect was to help sustain a network of support for the work of the Gardens on the part of some politically and socially influential landowners. Among the estates that Fred is known to have had contact with were

49

Kilmacurragh, County Wicklow, owned by the Acton family, notable for its conifers and rhododendrons; Mount Usher, County Wicklow, owned by the Walpole family, a prime example of a garden laid out in the naturalistic Robinsonian style; Mucklagh, near Aughrim, high up in the Wicklow mountains, one of the homes of Pierce O'Mahony, an alpine plant enthusiast; and Lissadell, in Sligo, owned

Edward Walpole in his garden at Mount Usher, County Wicklow. Sir Frederick Moore considered it 'the most interesting and edifying garden of its size in Ireland, if not in the British Isles'.

Sir Josslyn Gore-Booth and his wife Molly.

by Sir Josslyn Gore-Booth, the site of an extensive daffodil breeding programme.

Fred was in touch with less aristocratic gardening enthusiasts too, and on occasion he would write about their gardens. In August 1909 he visited Ashbourne, Glounthaune, County Cork, owned by Richard Beamish, a prominent brewer and local politician, who had converted an old quarry into a rock garden and created an artificial lake in which he grew rare water lilies. Fred thought his was 'one of the most interesting gardens in the south of Ireland for hardy shrubs, herbaceous plants and alpines', and he described in detail – in an article in *The Garden* – the impressive collection of plants he found there. Overall, he thought it 'a splendid example of what can be done in a comparatively short time when the owner takes a keen interest in his plants, and when both master and man [the man being his gardener, Mr Hume] work together in harmony.'[21] Sir Frederick Moore thought the other essential ingredient was money.[22]

William Gumbleton, an irascible correspondent and owner of a fine garden in Cobh, County Cork.

Another well known gardener who had connections with Glasnevin was William Gumbleton, an elderly Victorian gentleman who had been a friend of Frederick Moore's father, and who had a fine garden at Belgrove, in Cobh, County Cork. He was well connected to prominent gardeners and botanists abroad and was a noted authority on genera such as *Cortaderia*, *Begonia* and *Dahlia*.[23] He was also a man of strong opinions and did not take kindly to people who did not share them. He and Fred seem to have got on well enough, though, and Fred wrote a complimentary article about his garden after his visit in July 1909.

Of the many rare plants he found there, Fred was struck by Gumbleton's *Olearia insignis* (*Pachystegia insignis*), originally from New Zealand, which he thought 'one of the best in Britain growing in the open'; by his *Buddleja colvilei*, now over 20 feet high and 'producing trusses of its beautiful pink flowers'; and *Meconopsis chelidoniifolia*, a yellow flowering poppy from Szechuan, the first time Fred had seen one.[24]

Such a favourable write-up did not prevent Gumbleton from telling Fred on several occasions what he thought on other horticultural matters in his usual blunt manner, especially when he thought Fred got things wrong: 'I have seen your statement in *Irish Gardening*', he wrote in November 1910, 'that the two scandent aconites *A. Vilmorini* and A. *Latisectum* are one and the same plant. In this I think you are mistaken.'[25] There seem to have been no hard feelings, however. When Gumbleton died in 1911 Fred was able to make another visit to Belgrove and buy some of his plants for Glasnevin, although by the time he got there he found that the best of them were already gone. Of far greater value was Gumbleton's collection of rare botanical and horticultural books which he bequeathed to the library at Glasnevin.[26]

Fred also liked to travel outside Ireland. He was used to spending his annual leave travelling in Europe and he liked nothing better than to combine his holidays with collecting plants, especially alpines. The first of these trips for which there is a record was to Switzerland in 1909.

The snowbound lily pond at Glasnevin, February 1910 (CFB).

Saxifraga florulenta.

4

Botanizing in Europe

In June 1909 Fred joined a group which Rev. John Horsley, a canon of Southwark Cathedral in London and keen botanist, took each year to the Swiss Alps. He had the summer chaplaincy at the English church in Meirengen, and conceived the idea of organising healthy and uplifting holidays for those of modest means.[1] Fred may well have been on this trip before, since he had told a friend about it before deciding to join him on that summer's expedition. That friend was Reginald A. Malby. He was an authority on the domestic cultivation of alpine plants, had created a rock garden at his home in Woodford in Essex and then wrote a book about it, appealing to the growing number of alpine plant enthusiasts. He ran his family's photography business and was a highly accomplished plant photographer himself, securing appointments as official photographer to the Royal Horticultural Society and the Chelsea Flower Show.[2]

Malby wrote about this trip to Switzerland in his book, *With Camera and Rücksack: In the Oberland and Valais*, and illustrated it with his own photographs.[3] He has more to say about the flowers he found and the intricacies of taking photographs with the heavy apparatus he took with him than the people he was with, and he refers to Fred throughout as

*Rev. John Horsley, canon of South-
wark cathedral, keen naturalist and
organiser of an annual holiday to the
Swiss Alps. He is seen here with his
mayoral chain of office after being
elected mayor of Southwark in 1909.*

simply 'my companion'. Parts of it are redolent of George and Weedon Grossmiths' *Diary of a Nobody*. Malby nevertheless conjures up an evocative Edwardian world of plant-collectors and continental holiday-makers that would soon be no more. The First World War would put an end to organised expeditions of this kind, and plant-collecting was not nearly as popular as in its Victorian heyday.

Fred did not write an account of the trip, but he did recall one of its highlights several years later – the spectacular sight of *Saxifraga cotyledon* covering the mountainsides near the Grimsel Pass.

'To see this big Rockfoil growing naturally is a beautiful sight, its large pyramidal masses of white, crimson-spotted flowers waving in the slightest breeze elicits the admiration of passers-by.'

None of them, however, was within easy reach for Fred and Malby, and it looked as though they would be unable to get the photograph they wanted. Eventually, though, with Malby hanging on precariously to Fred's extended alpenstock, 'we found a place where, by scrambling over the parapet guarding the road, my companion, Mr Malby, was able to secure a photo of some rosettes'.[4]

What Fred didn't mention, though Malby did in his account, was that his photograph of the best of these specimens, for which he had used a large-scale negative, turned out to be 'quite blank'.

'Evidently I had been so absorbed in how I was to make the exposure that I had quite overlooked the matter of drawing the shutter of the dark-slide. Other photographers will, I am sure, appreciate the meekness of spirit which comes over one at such a time.'[5]

Reginald Malby, professional photographer, alpine plant enthusiast and Fred's companion in Switzerland in 1909. He would become a regular contributor to Irish Gardening.

Fred did better with his own camera. He took photos of the River Aare in flood at Meirengen, which Malby devotes a chapter to in his book; the Reichenbach Falls nearby, scene of the fictional Sherlock Holmes's vanquishing of his arch enemy Professor Moriarty; and some *Anemone narcissiflora* that he found at Aareschlucht, the Aare gorge.

The proprietors of Hotel Post, Meiringen, 1909.
From Fred's photograph album.

Two years later Fred's holiday took him further afield. His choice of destination arose from his contact with Pierce O'Mahony, owner of estate and gardens at Mucklagh, near Aughrim, and at Grangecon, County Wicklow. Mahony was an interesting character, a wealthy Protestant landowner and philanthropist who, unusually for somebody of his background, supported the Irish nationalist cause. He was a trained horticulturist and had a much admired rock garden and collection of alpine plants. He also kept a small alligator, brought to him from America, so Fred discovered on one visit, by John Redmond, the nationalist political leader.[6]

A defining moment in Pierce O'Mahony's life had been a visit to Bulgaria in 1903 on a relief mission, as a result of which he set up an orphanage in Sofia, and became friendly

Pierce O'Mahony (centre, with white beard), with the boys at the orphanage he founded in Sofia; and below in the uniform he devised for them to wear. Two of the boys would later be educated in Ireland.

with the German-born king of Bulgaria, Ferdinand I. A large inheritance from an extinct Russian branch of his family enabled him to pursue both philanthropic and horticultural interests. He also joined the Bulgarian Orthodox Church whilst retaining his membership of the Church of Ireland – and ended up a Roman Catholic.

'The O'Mahony' (as he liked to be known) was keen to populate his gardens with plants from Bulgaria, and he

Saxifraga cotyledon, and Fred's photograph (opposite) taken on a mountainside near the Grimsel Pass in the Swiss Alps in 1909.

asked Fred to help, agreeing to sponsor a plant-collecting expedition. Glasnevin's plant stock, it was understood, would be supplemented too.[7] For Fred it was in effect a subsidized holiday enabling him to do what he loved doing. His friend Herbert Cowley, by this time assistant editor of *The Garden* as well as editor of the *Kew Guild Journal*, joined the party as well.

The two of them arrived in Bulgaria on 16 June 1911. The O'Mahony was already there, and they met up at his orphanage in the capital, Sofia. As they sat outside in the courtyard, drinking coffee, and discussing the merits of Bulgarian sour milk, a car drew up. It came from the Royal Palace, with a message to say that the King, having heard about their arrival, would like to see them the next day. King Ferdinand was a keen botanist and gardener and, it turned out, had a particularly good collection of alpine plants in the royal gardens.

Their audience with the King did not begin propitiously, however. 'In the course of conversation,' Fred recalled, 'the King remarked that English nurserymen are doing their best to exterminate some rare plants,' and gave the example of *Lilium jankae*, a yellow mountain lily, which used to grow in abundance on the Vitosha mountain but had now virtually disappeared. Fortunately, Fred was able to reassure him that 'I had not come to strip the country ruthlessly of rare plants, but only wanted a few of each', and King Ferdinand promised

them 'every help and facility in the way of guides, ponies and even a railway carriage'.[8]

Accompanied by M. A. Delmard, Director of the King's Gardens, Ball and Cowley's first expedition took them to the nearby Vitosha mountain. Despite the depredations of earlier collectors they found much to interest them and Fred took plenty of photographs. He was particularly struck by the honey balm (*Melittis melissophyllum*), with its large pink

*Ferdinand I, King of Bulgaria, who Fred and
Herbert Cowley met in 1911.*

flowers, and *Geranium macrorrhizum*, which he was told was a
favourite flower among Bulgarians.

They spent one night on Mount Vitosha in a peasant's
hut. As darkness set in, so Cowley related, they approached a
local shepherd to ask if they could spend the night in his hut
or in one of his cattle shelters.

'On learning that we were English and Irish he took us
to his hut and made us welcome. Nothing,' Cowley thought,
'could have been more crude and primitive than this

Lilium jankae, *Bulgaria's yellow mountain lily –*
once at risk from English collectors.

dilapidated dwelling and yet it was the typical home of the
Bulgarian peasant.' The only form of decoration, they were
amazed to discover, was 'a portrait of Gladstone', revered as
a supporter of the Bulgarian cause, cut out and pasted on the
wall. 'The name of Gladstone is honoured above all others
by the Bulgarian peasants and they talk fondly of him.'[9]

Cowley thought they talked rather less fondly of their
current king. While Fred's published accounts of the trip
spoke warmly of the 'courtesy and kindness of the king and
queen' and of Bulgaria prospering under the king's 'intelligent
and wise rule', Cowley was not quite so enthusiastic – at
least in retrospect. He was struck by the contrast between the
'pomp and extravagance of court life', the king's 'ostentatious
show of wealth and lavish decoration' and the poverty of the
people. 'The country is poor, and signs of poverty are seen on
all sides. One does not need to be in Bulgaria long to realise
that King Ferdinand is far from popular with his subjects.'[10]

*The Vitosha mountain, Bulgaria, where Fred's party
commenced their plant collecting (CFB).*

A couple of days later, joined by The O'Mahony, they took the train to Stara Zagora, some 150 miles to the east of Sofia. Here they breakfasted on arrival at the Bishop's House (breakfast consisted of 'a cup of Turkish coffee and a cigarette'), then visited the king's beautiful gardens at Urana, and spent two days on the Belmeken mountain near Kostenets. Here, Fred noted, *Rhododendron myrtifolium* was especially in evidence and was quite distinct from the plant grown in English gardens under the same name.

On 21 June, accompanied by Herr Johann Kellerer, the King's Gardener, and a noted alpinist after whom several species and hybrids were named, the party travelled north, through the Shipka Pass and on to their destination, the Sokolski Monastery. They passed obelisks and trenches marking the spot where, in fierce battles against the

Turks, the Bulgarians had gained their independence. Fred 'came across a rather nice broom called *Genista spathulata*', but was struck far more by the 'glorious' sight of *Haberlea rhodopensis* (Orpheus flower), 'a blaze of colour', covering a rockface hundreds of feet high'.[11] As they searched about, noticing some plants that varied slightly in shades of colour and size of flowers, 'Herr Kellerer suddenly shouted out, "Weiss, weiss", in an excited tone', and came along bearing a lovely two-foot tuft 'covered with white flowers', a rare albino variety. The sight of these *Haberlea*, Fred wrote later, 'is one which was stamped on the memory'.[12]

Then it was on to the famous Valley of Roses, an area that stretched out over 80 miles, where nearly 170 villages cultivated roses for the supply of attar of roses

From top: Melittis melissophylum, Geranium macrorrhizum *and* Haberlea rhodopensis.

(distilled rose oil). After visiting the stills where the distilling took place, the party returned to Stara Zagora and from there went out to 'collect the quaint little *Iris mellita*', which grew in limestone ground, passing acres of *Rhus cotinus* (Venetian

Plant collecting in Bulgaria, probably near the Shipka pass.
Herbert Cowley is third from right on the white pony.
Below: Local girls gathering roses near Shipka, 1911. Fred
turned both images into lantern slides to illustrate talks and lectures.

sumach), which looked like 'a veritable field of flame', and made their way by train to O'Mahony's mountain home near Kostenets.

O'Mahony was again their guide as they travelled to the snow-topped Belmeken mountains. After three days collecting plants the party then went their separate ways. Cowley returned to England, O'Mahony to his mountain home while Fred set off on the final leg of his trip with Herr Kellerer, meeting up with him at Tchamouri. Heavy rain restricted their movements but they were able to visit the mountain homes nearby that belonged to the king and prince, and to collect more plants on the surrounding hillsides. On 2 July, despite the rain, they set out to climb Mount Musala, the highest mountain in Bulgaria, filling up their sacks along the way.[13] Herr Kellerer admired the 'neat little *Plantago gentianoides*', but the silvery leaf *Plantago argentea* appealed more to Fred, and he thought it well worth growing for its attractive foliage. After passing some *Primula deorum* (Rila primrose) as they continued their climb, they reached the summit and admired the 'glorious view' that stretched out as far as Macedonia to the southwest.

* * *

Fred followed up his trip to Bulgaria with two further expeditions – to the Maritime and Cottian Alps in France and Italy in 1912 and again in 1913. The first was sponsored by Sir Josslyn Gore-Booth, owner of Lissadell, County Sligo, and a good friend of Sir Frederick Moore. He was keen to add to his collection of alpine plants.

'Sir J. Gore Booth wants me to go to Switzerland about August 10th', Fred wrote on 22 July 1912, 'but would like to see me at Sligo first to make arrangements', adding that he

Primula deorum *and* Primula
allionii, *found in the Maritime Alps.*

expected it to be 'rather a warm job collecting on the mountaintops in the month of August'.[14]

In the event, the plan changed and Fred went not to Switzerland but to France and Italy. He told William Watson at Kew that he was 'taking his holidays to do some collecting (alpines) in the Cottian and Maritime Alps for Sir Josslyn Gore-Booth', and asked him if he could supply the name of 'any local botanist around Turin'.[15]

Watson seems to have obliged, for Fred wrote later of having received information 'forwarded by a local botanist' to the effect that the rare *Primula allionii*, in which he was particularly interested, could be found 'mostly in caves and grottos of the limestone cliffs' of the Maritime Alps in northern Italy.

When he got there he found that the best of them grew on the cliff face itself. 'Armed with a coal hammer and old chisel,' he wrote, 'I went to collect this *Primula*. A few accommodating plants may be levered out by the aid of a collector's strong trowel, but the majority are in minute cracks with roots delving deeply into the hard limestone without any soil, and standing on the cliff face, bathed in perspiration, with the scorching sun overhead, I soon understood why the plants have developed such a copious supply of glutinous and protective hairs.'[16]

Fred also made contact with another well known botanist in the region, Alwin Berger, curator of the Giardini Botanici Hanbury, the botanical gardens of the late Sir Thomas Hanbury at La Mortola, near Ventimiglia in north-west Italy. It seems Fred did then visit the famous gardens at La Mortola, and no doubt met up with Alwin Berger too, for among his surviving papers is a photograph he took of

Alwin Berger, curator of the Giardini Botanici Hanbury, La Mortola.

a seven-foot high *Agave franzosini* (Majestic Agave), marked 'La Mortola' on the reverse side, in his own hand.

This trip can be presumed a success as Fred returned to the same region the following year. This time he did write an account of it. He arrived in Turin on 11 August (accompanied by a friend, Mr H. M'Clenaghan), took the train to Cuneo and

A seven-foot high Agave franzosini *at La Mortola, from Fred's photograph album (1913).*

then the bus to the Valdieri thermal baths, where the 'large solitary hotel' was their base for exploration. The area was rich in flora but Fred was particularly struck by *Potentilla valderia*, which he thought would be 'well worth cultivating for their foliage, although the flowers are poor with small white petals'. Higher up the mountainside were some *Senecio incanus* (*Jacobaea incana*) which had a whiteness he thought unrivalled by any Alpine plant. His main objective in coming to Valdieri, however, was to collect seed of the rare *Viola valderia*, a pansy with grey-green leaves and lilac flowers with bright yellow centres. After a long search they did eventually find some growing but unfortunately the pods had already opened and the seeds were nowhere to be found. A 'terrific thunder storm of several hours duration' further depressed their spirits.[17]

(top to bottom, left to right): Viola valderia, Saxifraga florulenta, Eritrichium nanum, Viola nummariifolia.

The next day they hired a guide in order to help them find 'the home of that rare and difficult plant *Saxifraga florulenta*' and also *Viola nummulariifolia*, this granite region being the only area where the former was known to grow. They climbed higher up the mountain and into the Ciriega pass. Here they found the delicately-coloured *Viola nummulariifolia*, 'not only in hundreds but in thousands, sometimes peeping out from under huge blocks of stone or in loose tumbled granite, and some places even in gritty turf, where one could lift a clump a foot across'.[18]

Once through the pass they walked on, down the mountain, until they reached the Boreon Hotel in St Martin Vesubie, just over the border in France. This was to be their base for their primary target, *Saxifraga florulenta*. They found some under the shady side of a cliff, struck by the 'beautifully regular rosettes of incurving shiny green leaves without a trace of silver'. There were seed pods lying around but not with the seeds they were after.

They carried on up the mountain and at the summit were rewarded by the sight of *Androsace imbricata* (*Androsace helvetica*), 'growing in chinks in the solid rock without any soil at all, forming silvery cushions studded with tiny white flowers with pinking centres'; and *Eritrichium nanum*, La Reine des Alpes, 'some still bearing lovely blue flowers and others just ripening their seed'. Then it was back down again: 'Nothing for it but to retrace our steps, and already we have stayed out too late, for it is nearly 5 o'clock, and mists swirl around us, but luckily are not constant, and we find the river, which is a guide to us on our homeward journey.'

Frederick Moore observed that Fred had a particular interest in 'the study of plants and plant life in the conditions of nature', noting that in Bulgaria in particular he 'collected

'The top of the Ciriega Pass in August',
from Fred's photograph album (1913).

many interesting and rare plants, and brought back valuable information as to the conditions under which plants grew in that country'. Fred appreciated the importance of soil conditions, for example, in understanding what enabled plants to thrive in their native habitat.

When he returned home after his first trip to the Maritime Alps he brought back a sample from the limestone cliffs on which *Primula allionii* grew and asked an expert at the Royal College of Science to carry out a chemical analysis. What then struck him, after hearing that the pieces of rock had an unusually high calcium carbonate content, was how the plant nevertheless flourished in very different conditions at Glasnevin. 'Plants are adaptable beings,' he observed, 'and the more we experiment, the more we learn.'[19]

5

Editor of Irish Gardening

F red made the most of his life in Dublin. His job, especially
after being promoted to Assistant Keeper in 1907, suited
him well, giving him far more freedom than he would have had
at Kew if he had remained there – and much better facilities,
and a more congenial environment, than if he had ended up
in one of the colonies. England, and friends and family, were
within easy reach, while Ireland's mild climate provided
ideal conditions for the cultivation of plants introduced from
distant lands, not just its native species.

He lived in quite modest circumstances at 18 Marguerite
Road in Glasnevin, a short walk from the Gardens. When
he first arrived in Dublin the plan was for him to move into
the foreman's lodge, previously occupied by Parnell and his
family. However, the house was in dire need of renovation,
obliging him to find somewhere else to live while the work
was carried out.

In the event, Fred preferred to stay on at Marguerite
Road, allowing John Besant and his wife to move into the
foreman's lodge. His landlady was Mary Clarke, a widow,
who lived with her adult son and daughter, and had two
other boarders. Both men, according to the census in April
1911, were clerks in the civil service – one with the General

Post Office, the other with the Congested Districts Board which had offices in Dublin. Everybody in the house gave their religion as 'Catholic' except Fred, whose entry read 'Protestant, Church of Ireland'. From comments in several of his letters it is evident that he did not take religious belief, or at least denominational differences, all that seriously, so leaving behind the Methodism of his youth for the church of Dublin's Anglo-Irish community may not have been too hard a transition.

Fred had a busy social life. He played whist and bridge with friends, went to the theatre and cinema, and joined a language club to improve his French and German. He was a keen sportsman and a member of the Finglas Golf Club and the Glasnevin Lawn Tennis Club. During the summer months, he played for Glasnevin against other local tennis clubs, and for a while acted as the club's treasurer. The tennis club also used to organise whist drives and other social and fund-raising events in which he participated too. Occasionally he went skating.

But a good part of Fred's social life was connected to his work and he became involved in two of Dublin's leading scientific organisations, the Dublin Naturalists' Field Club and the Dublin Microscopical Club. Both brought amateurs and professionals together in the pursuit of scientific knowledge, part of a wider network that was supported by such institutions as the Royal Irish Academy, the Royal College of Science, the National Library, the botanical and zoological gardens and the museums.[1]

Fred was elected a member of the Dublin Naturalists' Field Club in July 1908 after being proposed by the President, Professor G.H. Pethybridge (a lecturer in botany at the Royal College of Science), and seconded by W.F. Gunn, another committee member. The meeting took place at the Wingfield Arms Hotel, Kilmessan, County Meath, at the end of the club's field trip to the nearby river Boyne, during which everybody had got soaked by the heavy rain.[2] Fred joined the committee the following year.

Organising these excursions to investigate and record local flora and fauna was one of the committee's main functions. 'Conductors', drawn from members with the relevant expertise, were appointed, and it was not long before Fred was called upon. On 16 October 1909 the excursion was to the Powerscourt Estate in Enniskerry, County Wicklow, and Fred led one of the two parties that set off from the nearby waterfall in search of fungi; the day ended with tea, a lecture and discussion about what the two parties had

The formal gardens at Powerscourt, County Wicklow.
The Powerscourt demesne was a popular destination for
field trips organised by the Dublin Naturalists' Field Club.

The waterfall at Powerscourt.

found, and then the 6.17 pm train back to Dublin.[3] The following September Fred was appointed conductor of an excursion to the Murrough, County Wicklow, a stretch of coastal wetland rich in plant life.[4]

Each year, in the autumn, the club also held an indoor 'conversazione' at the Royal Irish Academy. They were quite elaborate occasions. Evening dress was encouraged, the meetings were well attended, and members and visitors were invited to hear a lecture as well as to display their own exhibits.

In 1908 the lecture was on 'The camera in service of natural history', by Mr P. G. Dallinger, from the Omagh Field Club, and Fred had an exhibit on 'insectivorous plants'; the following year his exhibit was on 'odoriferous plants', with Rev. W.S. Green presenting a lantern slide show on 'Scenes in the West of Ireland'; the year after that, 1910, he displayed 'some photographs showing Alpine plants in their natural haunts', competing for attention with such other 'objects of scientific interest' as sharks' teeth, the eggs of a duck-billed platypus and the skull of a sabre-toothed tiger.[5]

There was considerable overlap in membership between the Naturalists' Field Club and the Microscopical Club, but the latter was much smaller, its meetings rarely attended by more than a dozen people, and was more specialised in its

Dr G. H Pethybridge and Professor George Carpenter, leading naturalists in pre-war Dublin, both members of the Dublin Naturalists' Field Club and the Dublin Microscopical Club.

focus. The Microscopical Club had an annual field trip but their regular meetings were largely devoted to the detailed examination and discussion of specimens, most often plants, fungi and fossils. Fred joined in October 1907, proposed by Frederick Moore, seconded by Dr G.H. Pethybridge, a committee member of the Microscopical Club as well as the Field Club. The entomologist George Carpenter, professor of zoology at the Royal College of Science, and David McArdle, Fred's colleague at Glasnevin, were among the club's office holders.

Over the next few years Fred attended many of their meetings, at times supplying exhibits or giving talks about the physiology of a variety of different plants, illustrating his presentations with specimens, photographs and microscopic slides. On one occasion his subject was the carnivorous *Utricularia prehensilis*, 'a curious little bladderwort from

Utricularia prehensilis, the subject of one of Fred's talks to the Dublin Microscopical Club.

South Africa'; another time it was 'a new epiphytal orchid called *Angraecum andersonii* [*Microcoelia caespitosa*], a native of the Gold Coast, West Africa', whose 'special interest' was that it was 'leafless, the aerial roots doing the work of attachment, absorption and assimilation of food'.[6]

So Fred became a part of the vibrant, quite close-knit Dublin scientific community that sustained both organisations and he came to know many of its leading figures. Foremost among them was Robert Lloyd Praeger, Ireland's most eminent naturalist and a prolific author. He was one of the founders and editors of the *Irish Naturalist*, a member of the committee of the Dublin Naturalists' Field Club, a frequent conductor of its field trips, and he took a keen interest in Fred's *Saxifraga* hybrids, a genus he had been investigating too.[7]

As well as expanding his range of social and professional contacts, Fred's involvement in the two clubs provided him with opportunities, among friendly and knowledgeable colleagues, to exchange information and to enhance his own expertise. He comes across, in the reports of meetings of the Microscopical Club, as somebody who was as fascinated by what the microscope could reveal of the cell structure of particular plants as he was devoted to the practical business of growing and caring for them.

Robert Lloyd Praeger, the leading Irish naturalist of his day,
seen here with his wife Hedwig.

While forging a new life for himself in Dublin Fred
kept in close touch with his family in England, which he
still called 'home'. This was no longer Loughborough as
his family had dispersed and gone to live elsewhere, but he
visited his brothers and sister regularly over Christmas and
Easter and sometimes joined them for summer holidays.
At one point he offered to make a home in Dublin for his
mother Mary, widowed since 1889, and his youngest brother
Herbert, who was in very poor health. However, they didn't
think Dublin's climate would suit him, so Mary and Herbert
went to live instead with his sister Constance after she had
married and moved to Chorlton-cum-Hardy, Manchester.

In 1911 there were two big events in Fred's life: he became
editor of the monthly journal *Irish Gardening*, and he fell in
love with the 19-year-old Alice Lane.

The National Library, central to the life of Dublin's scientific community. R.L. Praeger was a librarian here from 1892 to 1923.

The offer of the editorship of *Irish Gardening*, late in 1911, was a tribute to the name Fred had made for himself in the world of horticulture in Ireland during the five years he had been part of it. He had been a regular contributor of articles and photographs to the journal since 1907 and as Assistant Keeper at Glasnevin, enjoying the confidence of Sir Frederick Moore, the leading figure in Irish horticulture, was an ideal candidate for the job. This time the issue of not being Irish-born did not arise since it was not a civil service position, *Irish Gardening* being owned by its shareholders.

Irish Gardening had been started in 1906, just before Fred came to Ireland, and was edited by David Houston, professor of botany and horticulture at the Royal College of Science. It claimed to be 'the only journal entirely devoted to gardening in its special application to Irish conditions', and it considered itself 'the organ of progressive horticulture in Ireland', seeking to strengthen the relationship between 'practical horticulture and the sciences underlying it'. Its wider aim was 'to make gardening popular in every home in Ireland, and to help with timely information and advice for those who are attempting to make a livelihood out of gardening'.[8] All this for an annual subscription of three shillings, post-free.

Friends in high places: Sir Horace Plunkett, agricultural reformer, driving force behind the Department of Agriculture and Technical Instruction, and supporter of Irish Gardening.

The vacancy for a new editor arose when Houston left to become the editor of a new journal, the *Irish Review*. It was understood that Fred would have to work on *Irish Gardening* in his own time, not during his working hours at the Gardens. He received a modest 'honorarium' of £25 a year – though with the promise of more if he could increase its circulation. There was certainly scope to do this. *Irish Gardening* was well regarded and attractively produced but it often lacked variety and some thought it too academic. The 'wider and more intimate knowledge of practical gardening possessed by Mr Ball', the proprietors of the journal hoped, would bring about the changes needed to attract new readers, while Fred himself expressed the wish to 'improve and increase circulation if

Front cover of Irish Gardening, *March 1912, the third issue after Fred took over as editor.*

I can'.[9] His Kew contacts were likely to be useful both in increasing the number of subscribers outside Ireland and in bringing in new contributors.

Fred threw himself into his new duties, writing around to friends and colleagues to drum up articles. He was able to offer a small payment in return which must have helped as an incentive. Sir Frederick Moore agreed to supply the lead article in the first issue under Fred's editorship (January 1912), about his travels in America, and he contributed again on several occasions later in the year and in 1913.

Fred's friend Reginald Malby contributed numerous articles as well as photographs, his expertise on rock gardens an asset given their continued popularity with the gardening public. Fred could rely upon colleagues at Glasnevin, particularly John Besant, Rosamund Pollock and May Crosbie, to help out. Rosamund Pollock wrote a regular column under the title of 'Hints to Amateurs' or 'Hints to Novices'; later May Crosbie, one of the 'lady gardeners' at Glasnevin, took this on too. A regular feature, 'This month's work', its content determined by seasonal demands, was typically contributed by Andrew Campbell, gardener to Lord Ardilaun at St Anne's in Clontarf, and Levi Childs, gardener to the Earl of Meath at Kilruddery, Bray.

Other occasional contributors included Murray Hornibrook, a resident magistrate, who lived at Knapton, near Abbeyleix, who was a leading authority on dwarf conifers as well as a good friend (close enough for Fred to be invited to stay one weekend);[10] Robert Lloyd Praeger, who wrote about the *Arbutus*, 'most beautiful and most interesting of our native trees' in 1912, and about 'Grey-leaved rock plants' and 'Hardy Stonecrops' (twice) in 1913;[11] and Eric Brown, Fred's friend from Kew, who wrote several articles for him on 'Planting in Uganda', which may not have appealed to everybody. In return, Fred tried to find a suitable assistant for him in Uganda, consulting with Kew on the matter.[12]

There were quite a few articles on fruit farming. This was a branch of horticulture which the government, advised by Sir Frederick Moore, was keen to encourage, and recently appointed instructors were well placed to write about their work. Fred

Andrew Campbell, gardener to Lord Ardilaun at St Anne's, and a regular contributor to Irish Gardening; *and Murray Hornibrook, resident magistrate at Knapton, near Abbeyleix, an expert on dwarf conifers.*

himself became friendly with Christopher Pike, owner of the Baskin Hill Fruit Farm in Cloghran, a few miles outside Dublin, and often went to visit him and his wife and young family. Pike supplied an article on 'Pruning for Apples', aimed at beginners, in one of the first issues of *Irish Gardening* after Fred took over as editor.[13] Fred was not pleased at having to get involved, however, as an expert witness in a court case when called upon to estimate the cost of damage to his fruit trees and other crops after livestock from a neighbouring farm got in among them.[14]

Editing *Irish Gardening* meant a lot of time spent on correspondence, proofreading, visits to Falconers, the printers, at their offices in Upper Sackville Street, keeping track of payments to contributors and writing articles himself when gaps needed to be filled. He had to cut down on his social activities for time to do all this, but even then it was often a struggle to get everything done: 'up to 12 o'clock the last 3 nights' he wrote on 26 January 1912; another time it was back to the office after his supper and 'staying until about 11 to do more work'.[15] Much of Fred's 'extensive correspondence', Sir Frederick Moore thought, was carried on during 'what ought to have been hours of rest and recreation'.[16]

One of the many pages of advertisements in Irish Gardening *that helped to pay the bills.*

Fred's efforts paid off. No circulation details have survived but the large number of advertisements from commercial nurseries, seed merchants, suppliers of gardening equipment, greenhouses and the like suggest a confidence in *Irish Gardening* as an effective means of marketing their goods or services. Under Fred's editorship, Sir Frederick Moore wrote a few years later, the success of *Irish Gardening* 'was patent to every reader, and the high reputation which the Irish periodical is now held is largely due to his skill and enthusiasm'.[17] For the wider horticultural community at Kew and elsewhere, *Irish Gardening* was a showcase for what was being achieved across the Irish Sea.

And then there was Alice.

Alice Lane in 1913 or 1914.

6

Alice

Quite where and when Fred and Alice Lane first met remains a mystery. The tone of Fred's first letters in 1911 suggest they had known one another for a while, and a later letter mentioned his happy memories of visits to her family home and going out cycling together.[1] Tennis was a shared enthusiasm so that may have brought them together too. Alice was from a well-to-do Anglo-Irish family, originally from County Monaghan, who lived at No. 2 Charleville Terrace, North Circular Road, Phibsborough, a mile or so from Fred's more modest home in Marguerite Road in Glasnevin. She was the fourth of six children, and in 1911 she was 19 years old. Fred, at the end of that year, was 32.

Alice was a young woman of independent spirit, considered herself 'a lady by birth and education', and was not short of money.[2] Her father, Thomas Lane, a successful businessman with links to the Guinness brewery, had died at the beginning of 1911, leaving a considerable sum in the hands of trustees, along with instructions for the maintenance of Alice and her two younger brothers. The two boys, Stuart and Billy, were packed off to boarding school in England but this suited neither them nor the school (Cheltenham) and they were soon back

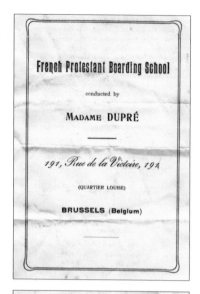

French Protestant Boarding School

conducted by

MADAME DUPRÉ

191, Rue de la Victoire, 191

(QUARTIER LOUISE)

BRUSSELS (Belgium)

Madame DUPRÉ receives a limited number of young ladies who desire a home abroad, where they can complete their education and acquire foreign languages. Special attention is paid to the household arrangements. The house, situated in the healthiest part of Brussels, is spacious and has a large and beautiful garden.

French is habitually spoken by all the household and Madame DUPRÉ is assisted by eminent professors and resident French, English and German governesses.

COURSE OF STUDIES

The course of instruction comprises the French, English, German and Italian languages, literature, history, elocution, history of fine arts, plain and fancy needlework.

TERMS

Board, including, warm baths and instruction in the above branches of knowledge, £ 80 for the scholastic year of ten months, payable in advance, viz :

15th September	£ 32
15th January	» 24
15th April	» 24

Brochure for Madame Dupré's French Protestant Boarding School, which Alice attended in 1911 and 1912.

in Dublin, their future a worry to all concerned, Fred included.

Alice and her mother, it seems, did not get on. This may help explain why, in September 1911, Alice took herself off to a finishing school in Brussels, enrolling in Madame Dupré's French Protestant Boarding School at 191 Rue de la Victoire.[3] Madame Dupré, according to her brochure, catered for 'a limited number of young ladies who desire a home abroad, where they can complete their education and acquire foreign languages'.

At a cost of £80 a year, not including extras, they could learn 'French, English, German and Italian languages, literature, history, elocution, history of fine arts, plain and fancy needlework'. It would help them, it was thought, to make a good marriage.

Alice would remain at Madame Dupré's school for the next 12 months. Apart from some bouts of homesickness at the beginning, she enjoyed her time there, became fluent in French and made some good friends among the other girls, most of whom came from continental Europe; she was the only one from Ireland. Once settled in she and

*A group of Alice's friends at Madame Dupré's school in Brussels.
Alice is sitting, second from left.*

Fred corresponded regularly and she kept all of his letters. Sadly, not one of her letters to him has survived, but if they had it seems they would have been rather fewer in number. He was the one making the running in their courtship, and several times he complained about her tardiness in replying. Once he said he thought that for every three letters he wrote he got one in reply.[4]

It is obvious from Fred's letters that he was smitten and he would shower her with compliments. They exchanged photographs. Sometimes he would send her plants and flowers, and even copies of *Irish Gardening*, hoping to interest her in his enthusiasms but worried that she might think this, and him, 'an awful bore'.[5] He was 12 years older than her and the age difference did show. He was ready to offer advice, for example, about photography which she was trying her hand at ('I don't think you gave the photos a long enough exposure'), and there were some things he disapproved of her doing – like smoking cigarettes, which she told him about on one occasion (he himself smoked a pipe).[6] Nor was he keen that she should go off and train as a nurse, which she contemplated at one point, obviously concerned that he might lose her.

Fred undoubtedly reflected the attitudes of many other men at this time. A case in point was his response to the incident in 1913 when English suffragettes, seeking to publicise their cause, caused consternation at Kew Gardens, damaging the orchid house and burning down the tea house.

'Did you see what the suffragettes are doing at Kew Gardens? Hope you have not turned one, for if any do damage here we are going to dip them all in the pond. So you will know what to expect, it will be worse than being caught on a fence.'

Alice sitting up in bed in her room at Madame Dupré's, 1911.
A photograph of Fred can be seen on the wall behind her.

*The tea house at Kew Gardens before it was burnt down
by militant suffragettes in 1913.*

But Fred's letters were amusing and informative and Alice loved getting them. He responded to news of her doings in Brussels and told her of his – about his work, including his dealings with 'the boss', Sir Frederick Moore; about the trials and tribulations of editing *Irish Gardening* ('I find its one thing getting the promise and another thing receiving the article');[7] about tennis and golf, about the films and plays he had seen; about the whist drives or games of charades with mutual friends. He often described his travels in Ireland and England. In May 1912, he told her about his trip to London to attend the Royal International Horticultural Exhibition, precursor of today's annual Chelsea Flower Show, and how he managed to get in for free with a press ticket.

'I was told I was not eligible for these [free tickets] so then I put in for a Press ticket as editor of the renowned

ROYAL INTERNATIONAL HORTICULTURAL ≋≋ ≋ ≋ ≋ EXHIBITION

MAY 22ⁿᵈ-30ᵗʰ 1912 ROYAL HOSPITAL GARDENS, CHELSEA

Publicity stamp advertising the Royal International Horticultural Exhibition in London in May 1912. Fred attended free of charge as the accredited representative of Irish Gardening. *He thought it was 'a scene of indescribable beauty'.*

Irish paper "I.G." and to my surprise and joy I received a complimentary ticket admitting me every day of the show, that's good isn't it. I'm coming to the conclusion there's nothing like cheek in this world and wished I was blessed with more of it.'[8]

He told Alice about his family too – about the death of his younger brother Herbert, after his long illness; about his mother Mary 'who always considered herself least', about his sister Connie and her husband Arthur and their new house, about another brother in Kent he had just visited, whose wife was 'a very jolly soul', though he thought she talked too much.[9]

Fred was always trying to find ways of meeting up with Alice. If he were come to Brussels, he wondered, 'would they let me see you without being guarded by half a dozen teachers?' Another time, early in 1912, he tried to persuade her to go and stay with Connie in Manchester so they could meet up there, suggesting she concoct a pretext that 'she wished to see a real busy manufacturing city in England to see how this compared to the Irish: you know you can spin a fine yarn when you like'.[10]

He tried to get her to go on holiday with him. In 1912 Reginald Malby had written to Fred to ask if he would go to the Pyrenees with him, a reprise of their time in Switzerland in 1909. But he told Alice he much preferred to go with her and her companion, Miss Colgan, on Canon Horsley's Swiss trip, if they would come. This 'is a really jolly affair and most of the party very nice people, you would thoroughly enjoy it, will you go?' The answer, it appears, was that she wouldn't, so Fred went off instead that year to collect plants in France and Italy. In the same letter he told her about the arrival at Glasnevin of 'Miss Watt, a Scottish lady gardener', going to see a popular new play called *The Girl in the Train*, playing a round of golf on Sunday afternoon, and finally an evening spent 'in thinking of and writing to the dearest, sweetest and best little girl in the continent'.[11]

They teased one another in their letters – Fred would complain she was 'humbugging' him – and he was ready to make fun of himself too. 'I'm really only a moderate kind of [tennis] player', he admitted, and told an embarrassing story of how he managed to hit himself on the face with his racket, rather than the tennis ball.[12] Another time he described how he had been due to give a lecture on his trip to Bulgaria but forgot to bring both his lecture notes and the attar of roses which he intended to give as a prize in the raffle that followed. He had to rush back to his digs to get them, arriving ten minutes late and leaving everybody wondering what had happened to him – 'I suppose you will say just like me,' he commented.[13]

Their long distance relationship, interspersed by occasional meetings in England and Ireland, had its ups and downs. Fred was always keen but Alice had her doubts and she kept putting him off visiting Brussels. But he was not deterred, and early in 1912 he wrote to her to propose. He told her he loved her dearly, but thought it was 'only right to tell you that I'm not well off, only enough to live quietly. Total income only comes to £220 or £230 a year including salary, interest on capital and I.G. work, but salary improved a little each year'.

Alice was not quite ready for this and wrote back to tell him so.

'I thought at one time you did care,' Fred wrote in response; 'but you say you don't know your own mind.' He quite understood, he said, and did not wish to persuade her against her will. 'I don't even wish you to think of saying yes under these circumstances. So now please don't think or worry about it any more, for it can't be helped and please don't say any more about it. We can still be friends as before and hope we will always be so. Finis.'[14]

But it seems relations were soon restored. They met up at Fred's sister's house in Manchester in July and Fred came away hopeful. 'I enjoyed the Manchester weekend and hope you did too. It was a real treat to see you again looking so well and jolly, improved in every way and prettier than ever, but I mustn't say too much or it might raise the "bumps of vanity."'

After leaving Brussels in the summer of 1912 Alice spent the autumn at a second finishing school, in Southport, run by Miss Baverstock, an establishment that was more concerned with practical matters of 'housecraft' than languages and fine arts. Fred and Alice saw a lot more of each other once Alice returned to Dublin at the end of the year and they grew closer. Alice was reconciled with her mother Sophia, and at one point considered sharing a house with her, but decided to live instead with a Mrs Flora Butler, probably an aunt or family friend, at 6 Grosvenor Place, Rathgar, south of the river.[15] Sophia, given the status-conscious Anglo-

Irish community to which she belonged, may have hoped for a more socially advantageous match for her daughter, but she liked Fred – everybody did – and on several occasions she came with Alice to see him at the Gardens.

EVERSLEY COLLEGE OF
HOUSECRAFT,
SOUTHPORT.

Principal :—Miss E. M. Baverstock, B.Sc. (Lond.)

Thorough training in well equipped building and on practical lines, in all domestic work, for educated girls over the age of seventeen.

The College is worked in connection with Eversley School, and students, therefore, have every opportunity of wide and varied experience during their training, and of continuing any special courses in Music, Art, Foreign Languages, etc., that may be desired.

Prospectuses may be had on application.

*Eversley College of Housecraft,
Southport, which Alice
attended in 1912.*

Another time Fred invited Alice to come for afternoon tea but was in a quandary as to what to do afterwards. His problem was one of conflicting loyalties. Sir Frederick Moore, he told her, was lecturing on botany from 7.00 pm to 9.00 pm in the evening: 'Its two long hours. If you would care to attend I would ask him for permission for you. But please understand I don't need to press you (in this sense) to go to the lecture unless you like, its just as you please. We could do something else or go somewhere here. If you have anything else on don't worry about coming here'. Whether she came or not is unrecorded, but attending a two hour lecture on botany from Sir Frederick Moore may not have been her idea of a night out.[16]

In March 1913 Fred proposed again. This time the answer was yes. Friends and family on both sides were delighted. Connie, by now a good friend, was excited by the prospect of having 'a new sister'.[17] Fred told Alice he had received 'a very nice letter from your ma, wishing us happiness etc', while his mother Mary wrote to Alice to say how delighted she was too: 'The news that letter contained will make my joyful Easter doubly joyous; to think that you are going to be my good Fred's companion for life and that, when I am gone, he will never be left lonely or unloved'. Fred had to face 'a very strenuous training', she added, 'but he bore it bravely and now we are all proud of his skill, and thankful that his warm heart remains the same.'[18]

Colleagues at Glasnevin offered congratulations too. Rosamund Pollock 'gave me a good slap on the back and "That's right" etc', while Sir Frederick Moore 'gave me a good handshake and told me it was the best thing I could do. Then he said, "What is she like?" I told him who you were and he said he remembered Tom Lane very well in the same boat rowing together.'[19] He and Alice's father, it turned out, had been at Trinity College Dublin at the same time. Sir Frederick would already have had Fred in mind as his successor so the likelihood that he would now be settling down in Dublin, marrying the daughter of a Trinity man and no doubt starting a family must have come as welcome news.

Alice Lane in 1913 or 1914.

One person who did not think it such a good idea was Constance Noar, a young English teacher at Madame Dupré's school in Brussels who had remained a close friend of Alice. 'Well now, I ought to offer you some positive form of congratulation, what shall I say? I think you are a silly kiddie to bind yourself at such a young age, but after all, bondage in some cases is very sweet and I hope yours will be'.[20]

Fred and Alice must have agreed a time for their wedding later in the year, and they considered where to live. Fred looked at houses in Ballymun Road and Iona Crescent in Glasnevin, and then Glasnevin Hill, but with no luck. The last was the worst, 'a rotten hole and not the sweet nest' he would like to begin their married

Constance ('Connie') Ohlson, Fred's sister, later in life.

life.[21] He spoke to 'Mr Strain the builder' who had built a number of new houses in Ballymun Road, but it turned out they had all been sold.[22] Fred also put his case to Professor James Campbell, assistant secretary at the Department of Agriculture and Technical Instruction (and brother-in-law of Sir Frederick Moore), in the hope that a house might be provided for them, but had no joy here either: 'at present the Treasury will not spend more than is absolutely necessary', he was told.[23]

But then, perhaps mindful of Constance Noar's words, Alice said she wanted to put off the wedding. Fred accepted this reluctantly, saying that 'if you would really like to wait a little longer we can do so, say till spring [1914] or whenever suits you'. On 2 July, Fred wrote to Alice, who was in

England, saying he had told his mother about 'the postponing of wedding and [had] asked her to tell Connie and Arthur'.[24] Once she was back in Dublin Alice contemplated getting a job as a lady's companion, which didn't come to anything, and then spent some more time in England, some of it with Connie and Arthur in Manchester.

At that point their story disappears from view. A brief letter of Fred's dated 2 August 1913 conveys the mundane news of a visit he had to make to the printers in connection with *Irish Gardening*, but then there is a gap of over a year until the next surviving letter. During this time they remained engaged but they did not take the next step. Fred continued to live in digs at Marguerite Road while Alice divided her time between relatives and friends in England and Mrs Butler's residence in Rathgar.

Fred, meanwhile, carried on with the job he loved at the Royal Botanic Gardens.

7

Botanist of Gough Barracks, The Curragh

Ireland's turbulent politics rarely impinged upon the work of the Royal Botanic Gardens, and Fred's letters to Alice never went much beyond their preoccupation with one another. Once there was a brief comment about the effects of the lock-out in 1913, mostly to express relief that he had managed to escape the worst of the disruption caused by the dispute. But the world around them was changing. In 1913 and 1914 Ireland was set on a course towards home rule and the necessary legislation, after years of campaigning by Irish nationalists, finally made its way through the British Parliament. Protestant Ulster resisted and threatened violence but failed to derail the process. Some, however, thought civil war was only a matter of time.

But the storm clouds had yet to break. At the Botanic Gardens, whatever the tensions elsewhere, it was a time of relative stability, sufficient funding and strong leadership. Continued government support for horticulture and forestry, alongside agriculture, underlined the importance of the work that Fred and his colleagues carried out at Glasnevin, and the Department of Agriculture and Technical Instruction drew upon their expertise. Sir Horace Plunkett, the architect of much of this, may have been driven by a bigger political purpose – the doomed hope of saving the union – but there was no doubting the transformation he brought about, nor the improvement in Ireland's finances, that took place in the years before 1914.

Fred had a growing reputation in his field. He was invited to give a lecture to the Royal Horticultural Society in London about his plant-collecting trip to Bulgaria and then had it published in the Society's journal.[1] He was a member of the Kew Guild committee, representing horticulturists in Ireland, and was involved in the formation of an Irish branch.[2] He corresponded regularly with leading botanists and horticulturists. As well as his former colleagues at Kew, these included Richard Irwin Lynch, curator of the Cambridge University Botanic Gardens, whom he had visited in 1913; W.R. Dykes, a master at Charterhouse School in Surrey who was considered the world's leading authority on irises; and E.A. Bowles, owner of Myddelton House and its famous garden in Enfield, Middlesex, with whom Fred had been in touch – usually about crocuses – since 1907. The two would have met during Bowles's visits to Ireland and it was Bowles who chaired the meeting at the Royal Horticultural Society in February 1913 when Fred delivered his lecture on 'Botanizing in Bulgaria'.[3]

Closer to home, from 1913, was the eminent figure of Augustine Henry who Fred would have remembered from his time at Kew – and indeed from a couple of Kew Guild dinners subsequently when he was guest of honour. Since then Dr Henry had moved to Cambridge to help establish a new school of forestry, and co-authored an encyclopaedic account of trees in Britain and Ireland. Originally from

County Tyrone, he returned to Ireland in 1913 to take up the new chair of forestry at the Royal College of Science, an initiative funded by the Department of Agriculture and Technical Instruction.[4] Once in Dublin he was in regular contact with the Botanic Gardens, meeting and corresponding with both Fred and Sir Frederick Moore when the need arose, and always ready to share his expertise. Several of his letters to Fred survive, setting out his detailed replies to Fred's queries about different

Professor Augustine Henry (standing) with Henry Elwes, his co-author on The Trees of Great Britain and Ireland.

tree species at Glasnevin. On occasions Fred would make the necessary arrangements, and provide plant specimens, when Henry came to the Gardens with his students, or when attending meetings of the Irish Forestry Society.[5]

Fred was always ready to welcome humbler visitors to Glasnevin too. 'Naturally I came to know C.F. Ball and his successor, J.W. Besant,' wrote Bertram Anderson, a young alpine plant enthusiast living in Sandymount who often spent his Saturdays at the Gardens, 'and many plants came to my little garden from the generosity of these people.'[6]

Irish Gardening continued to flourish and Fred could draw upon a growing network of friends and colleagues for the articles he needed. In these circles, Sir Frederick Moore said, he 'was regarded as a sound authority on many branches of horticulture, his opinion and advice being constantly sought and freely given'.[7]

Somehow he found the time to write for other gardening journals besides his own. He was at his best when providing detailed descriptions of plants at Glasnevin. A piece he wrote for the *Gardeners' Chronicle* in July 1914 about *Globularia incanescens*, a dwarf hardy perennial, was a typical example. He described its features, told his readers of its origins in the Mediterranean region, and what he thought about its qualities. Most of these globe daisies, he said, 'can scarcely be classed as choice or first-class rock plants', but *Globularia incanescens* was an exception, 'a real gem', and he loved its pale blue flowers. 'There is something so charming in its fluffy, globular flower heads, neat and compact habit, that this *Globularia* wins praise from all lovers of Alpines who have seen it.'[8] Knowledge and enthusiasm come across in equal measure. Often his articles were illustrated with his own black and white photographs.

Fred was also 'keenly interested in hybridisation', Sir Frederick Moore said, 'and conducted several interesting

Globularia incanescens, one of many plants at Glasnevin which Fred wrote about in Irish Gardening, Gardeners' Chronicle *and other journals.*

experiments with much success'. In 1913 and 1914 this work came to fruition. One of these 'interesting experiments' produced *Calceolaria × ballii*, a slipperwort with sulphur-yellow flowers, created from two Peruvian parents, *C. deflexa* and *C. forgetii* (*C. virgata*). *C. deflexa* was quite common in Ireland, but *C. forgetii* only came to Glasnevin from Kew in October 1912. Fred sowed seed from the fertilised flowers in March 1913, and the first flowers of the hybrid opened in December. He described the result, in an article in the *Gardeners' Chronicle*, as 'a pretty little greenhouse shrub, and almost intermediate in character between its two parents'. Since he gave his name to it he must have been pleased with the outcome.[9]

Another of his successful hybrids was a bell-flower, *Campanula reineri × pusilla*, most likely derived from plants Fred had brought back from the mountains of Europe. According to John Besant, Fred created several such crosses in the summer of 1914. When they eventually flowered two years later the same cross produced seedlings that differed significantly from one another in their characteristics, one of them being closer to *C. pusilla*, the other to *C. reineri*. Besant thought the latter was the best, 'a beautiful bell-flower, light rosy lilac in colour, with larger leaves than either of its parents'.[10]

Calceolaria × ballii, *a hybrid slipperwort with yellow flowers which Fred gave his name to in 1913.*

Most successful of all were the hybrid cultivars Fred created from *Escallonia*, a South American evergreen shrub. Three variants resulted from these crosses. One was simply known as 'Glasnevin hybrid', with dark green leaves, rare today, but still extant. The second, with larger flowers, red-pink in colour, and glossy green leaves, Fred named after Alice, then his fiancée. The

Campanula reineri × pusilla, *a bell-flower, one of Fred's successful hybrids.*

third, *Escallonia* 'C. F. Ball', with blood-red petals and bright gold stamens, would become the best known and longest lasting, but only acquired its name after Fred's death.[11]

George Smith, of the Daisy Hill Nursery, implied that he was instrumental in this. Years later he recalled how in 1914, when 'looking round the then "Royal" Botanic Gardens with the late Mr Ball, he showed me some seedling *Escallonias*, the result of some crosses he had made, and said that one was

Escallonia *cultivars which Fred created at Glasnevin: (top)* Escallonia 'Glasnevin hybrid'; *(bottom)* Escallonia 'Alice'.

a rather good one. His offer of a few cuttings was gladly accepted, and these were grown on under the title "*Escallonia* C.F. Ball", and eventually developed into fine specimens, proving it to be, in my estimation, the finest and brightest of the family'.

This account, however, written twenty years later, does not quite tally with the fact that the earliest record (in the Glasnevin donations register) of cuttings of 'C.F. Ball' being sent to George Smith was October 1920.[12] So it may be that *Escallonia* 'C.F. Ball' was actually named and developed at Glasnevin well before Mr Smith made a commercial success of it at the Daisy Hill Nursery. On the face of it, given the esteem in which Fred was held by his colleagues at Glasnevin, and the existence since

*Escallonia 'C.F. Ball', showing its distinctive blood-red flowers.
It acquired its name only after Fred's death. George Smith,
proprietor of the Daisy Hill nursery in Newry, considered it
'the finest and brightest of the family'.*

1913 or 1914 of *Escallonia* 'Alice', that does seem likely. What could have been more natural than them wishing to honour him in this way?

*   *   *

In August 1914 the era of peace in Europe came to an end. The assassination of the Archduke Franz Ferdinand in Sarajevo, then part of the Austro-Hungarian Empire, set in train a series of events which led to war between the principal European powers. Ireland's home rule crisis was subsumed within a larger world crisis and it was agreed that home rule would be postponed until after the war. Reactions to Britain's declaration of war reflected Ireland's longstanding divisions. Many, including a majority of those who had been pressing for home rule, expressed support for the British side in the impending conflict with Germany and her allies. Others were opposed, thought Ireland should keep out of the conflict, or saw in this crisis the opportunity to press for full independence at a time when Britain's resources would be stretched to the limit.

In Dublin, stronghold of Ireland's Anglo-Irish community, there were patriotic demonstrations and young men came forward to enlist in Irish regiments such as the Royal Irish Fusiliers, the Royal Munster Fusiliers and the Royal Dublin Fusiliers. The 7th Battalion, Royal Dublin Fusiliers, the destination for a volunteer corps raised within days of the outbreak of war by the Irish Rugby Football Union, attracted the most attention. Many of its recruits were well known rugby players and drawn from the ranks of civil servants, barristers, solicitors, bankers, stockbrokers and the like – the cream of Dublin society, at least as seen by unionist newspapers like *The Irish Times*. They were constituted as a

Recruiting for the Royal Dublin Fusiliers in the autumn of 1914.

Recruitment posters that circulated in Ireland in the autumn of 1914.

'pals' battalion, enabling all who enlisted together to serve in the same battalion, rather than being allocated to several different ones. They would, in the words of the commanding officer, 'Mess', 'drill', and work together, and I hope, fight the common enemy together'.[13] 'D' company, 7th Battalion, was to be reserved, although not exclusively, for volunteers from the Irish Rugby Football Union. They soon came to be known simply as 'The Pals'.

Fred was not among this initial batch of recruits but applied to join some weeks later. In a letter to Alice on Friday, 6 November, he said, 'So far I haven't heard anything about my application,' and made arrangements to play golf with her that weekend, weather permitting. 'Wear the strongest pair of boots you have to play golf,' he advised, 'never mind what they look like.'[14]

News of his application came a few days later. His next letter to Alice, dated 20 November, was headed 'B company,

RDF', and sent from the army's training base at the Curragh, County Kildare, some 30 miles from Dublin. He began it by asking Alice to 'Excuse scribble but its a job to write here as there's always a row'.[15] Four days later he wrote again but this time his letter was headed 'D company, RDF, The Curragh', so it seems he had secured a transfer.[16] He was now in with the rugby players, some of whom he knew, nearly all of them from educated, professional and protestant backgrounds. Like them he joined as a private and had not sought a commission.

'Only those who knew him well,' one of Fred's friends wrote later, 'will ever thoroughly appreciate how much he gave up and what a wrench it was to him to throw up the work he loved so well.'[17] Not only his work: he was of course engaged to be married too. It would have been understandable, in these circumstances, if he had hesitated.

Eugene Duffy, foreman gardener to the Earl of Meath at Kilcuddery, Bray, before he enlisted in the Royal Dublin Fusiliers.

For a few weeks, until the age limit for new recruits was raised from 30 to 35, he couldn't have done so anyway. But as an Englishman in Ireland, identifying with its Anglo-Irish community, he would have felt duty bound to serve King and Country. Other men at the Botanic Gardens felt the same way. One of the first to leave his job to enlist was William Lacey, the caretaker, who rejoined the Royal Irish Fusiliers on 31 August. A veteran of the Anglo-Boer War of 1899–1902, he had 25 years' service in the army behind him – and had only been working at the Gardens for a few months when war broke out.

Friends and colleagues elsewhere were enlisting too: horticulturists like Eugene Duffy, foreman gardener to the Earl of Meath at Kilruddery, Bray;[18] Freemasons from the Shakespeare Lodge in Dublin, which Fred had joined earlier in the year; and in England, fellow Kewites like Herbert Cowley, his companion on the trip to Bulgaria, who joined the County of

Sir Frederick Moore and son Freddie, 11 years old at the outbreak of war.

London Regiment in September 1914. Closest to Fred, though, of those who answered the call to arms, was his younger brother Wilfred – now living in Leicestershire and married with two small children – who joined the 12th Lancers, a cavalry regiment, at the end of August.[19]

A story has been passed down at Glasnevin that Fred enlisted with the Royal Dublin Fusiliers after being sent a white feather, a symbol of cowardice and part of a campaign to shame young men not in uniform to enlist. The story was told, later in life, by the late Major General Frederick Moore, son of the Keeper, Sir Frederick Moore, and it was based on his memories of what he had heard many years earlier – either at the time of the incident (when he was eleven years old) or after it.[20]

There is no independent verification of his claim but there seems no reason to doubt his memory. Fred Ball would have been a familiar figure to him, and over 70 years later he remembered exactly where his office was. And it was indeed the case that women were active in this pernicious white feather campaign in the weeks and months after the outbreak of the war, in Dublin as in other parts of Britain and the empire.

But whether, if we allow that Moore's memory was accurate, being the recipient of a white feather had any effect on Fred's decision to enlist, or its timing, it is impossible to know. Given Fred's situation, and the example of others around him, it was always likely that he would respond to the call to serve his country when it came. The incident may in any case have taken place after he had applied to join the Fusiliers, and while his application was still being processed,

In military uniform at the Botanic Gardens, late 1914 or early 1915.

in which case it could have had no bearing on his decision. A reasonable conclusion, given what we know of Fred's circumstances, and of Fred himself, is that it did not require a white feather to persuade him that enlisting was the right thing to do, however much he stood to lose by doing so. The fact that he chose to join a local regiment, rather than return to England to enlist, was a clear indication of where his loyalties now lay.

*   *   *

Several letters of Fred's to Alice survive from the days and weeks after he joined the Fusiliers, all of them written from the Curragh. In one, he thanked her for sending him some shoes, brushes and warm clothes, but asked her to make sure that next time she wrote his name clearly, and add his regimental number (16445), as 'there are several names like Bell and Bull and your Sunday's letter wandered off in another room but fortunately was not opened'.[21]

In another, he asked if she might like to come to visit him one Saturday, suggesting the train to Newbridge Station and then a short cab ride – since the Curragh was 'not much of a place for ladies' he thought she should bring a companion too.[22]

Alice wondered what Fred and his fellow recruits actually did all day. This was his answer: 'You wanted to know what we do, well we are awakened at 6 o'clock, dress and make our beds etc. to be on parade at a quarter to 7. We drill usually without rifles until quarter to 8, get breakfast and turn out with rifle for another hour, then after 10 minutes rest we do 2 hours gym (Swedish) and then in our short sleeves we go for a run or walk, for ½ or ¾ of an hour, then get dinner, turn out again ¼ to 2, sometimes more gym or a march and

Alice Ball, c. 1920.

finish up for tea about 5 o'clock. After tea we (the recruits) sometimes have to go to the rifle range for practice. For the evening usually go to get a cheap supper at one of the soldiers' homes.'[23]

These letters also reveal that they had decided to get married. Alice had previously been the one wishing to delay but now she wanted to go ahead as soon as possible, particularly after Fred told her of rumours that his battalion might be sent 'to the south of France towards the end of January or beginning of February'.

'Your proposal to be married early,' he told her on 24 November, 'would be ideal for me and then we might have one or two glorious weekends together, it would be like paradise after the barracks.' Since there was another rumour 'that we are getting leave half of us at Xmas and the other half the New Year,' he asked her, 'would either of those suit you for the wedding, I don't know yet how long we get.'

In the event they didn't have to wait that long. Fred applied for and was granted special leave, and they were married on Saturday 16 December in Holy Trinity Church, Rathmines, close to where Alice was living. On the torn and battered wedding certificate that survives, Fred is described as a 'botanist' of 'Gough Barracks, Curragh Camp', and Alice as 'spinster' of '6 Grosvenor Place, Rathmines'. They were married by licence, according to the rites and ceremonies of the Church of Ireland, by the Rev. Ernest Lewis Crosby, the rector of Rathmines, and a friend of Alice's family. Alice's mother Sophia was present as a witness, as was Robert

13 platoon, 'D' Company, 7th battalion, Royal Dublin Fusiliers, 1914/15. Fred is in the third row back, 5th from right.

Scholefield, the family solicitor and trustee for her late father's estate.

For Fred it was only a brief interlude from his military training: he had to be back at the barracks on the Sunday evening. So much for any ideas of a romantic honeymoon.

Alice had been busy finalising arrangements for the rented house they had found. Fred wrote to say, 'My little darling, you can just arrange the house as you think best'; 'the arrangements you suggest for bedrooms will suit me very well', but he thought that having the room that led into the greenhouse as the drawing room 'will be favourite as it is the most pleasant room'. He was pleased to hear that a good friend of theirs, Mrs Horan, was happy to provide some advice, 'she is a jolly decent sort and sensible at the same time'.[24] Their house, 'Melville', a former rectory, was in Ballymun Road, Glasnevin – just a short walk from the Gardens.[25] They cannot have spent very many days there together.

The Royal Dublin Fusiliers remained at the Curragh until 2 February 1915 when they were transferred to the Royal Barracks in Dublin, the site of today's National Museum. That weekend Fred made a will, leaving everything to Alice, save the sum of £22 a year to be paid to his mother during her lifetime. It was witnessed by two men who had by now become good friends, fellow 'D' Company Fusiliers, privates Cecil Gunning and Frank Laird.

Cecil Gunning was from a large family in Enniskillen, County Fermanagh, and educated at the prestigious Portora Royal School. When war broke out he was 22 years old and working as a clerk in the Belfast Savings Bank in Pettigo, County Donegal. A signatory of the Ulster Covenant in 1912, and opposed to home rule, he would have seen enlisting in the Fusiliers as his patriotic duty, his contribution not just to the defeat of Germany but to the preservation of the union. He was joined by his younger brother Douglas (Frank as he was usually called) who worked for another bank, the Bank of Ireland in Sligo. When he was refused leave of absence so he could enlist, he left anyway, cycling all the way to Enniskillen before getting the train to Dublin.[26]

The second witness to Fred's will was Frank Laird, who became his closest friend. Frank was a civil servant in Dublin (a self-described 'pen-pusher'), son of a Methodist minister, the same age as Fred and just as unlikely a soldier. He considered himself to be 'naturally a man of peace', but had

Soldiers of No. 2 section, 13 Platoon, Royal Dublin Fusiliers.
Frank Gunning (standing) and his elder brother Cecil (sitting)
are highlighted. Hugh Anderson is standing at the end
of the row, right-hand side. Sitting, in the middle, is Sgt. Norman
Wood, soon to be replaced as section leader by Sgt. R.S. Sutcliffe.
The photograph was taken in February 1915.

Frank Laird, Fred's closest colleague in the Fusiliers.

concluded, after considerable heart searching, that he ought to join up; he worried, he said, about 'how my friends would regard me afterwards if they found me still at home when the war was over'. The two obviously got on very well, kindred spirits among mostly younger and more boisterous colleagues. Frank called Fred his 'chief friend', thought him 'silent and reserved' but added that 'it did not take a very long acquaintance to find the kindliness that lay behind his modest bearing, and the strength that made him a man not to be trifled with'.[27]

Fred, Frank and the two Gunnings were in No. 2 section, 13 platoon – 12 men led by a non-commissioned officer – and they developed into a close-knit unit. They were known colloquially as 'The Guinness Grenadiers', according to Cecil Gunning, because five of their number were employed by the brewery before they enlisted. Their section leader was Lance-Corporal Norman Wood, another Portora Royal School old boy – and one of the Guinness five. He would soon be promoted to sergeant and then transferred to 'A' Company, his place taken by Sgt R.S. ('Suttie') Sutcliffe, the regimental heavyweight boxing champion.[28]

The regime at the Royal Barracks 'caused no slackening in the intensive training', Frank Laird wrote, and they spent much of their time at Flanagan's Quarry, 'about five miles outside Dublin', practising trench-digging. Here they found 'an elaborate system (it seemed to us) of trenches and dugouts

(top) Resting on a route march outside Dublin;
(bottom) Soldiers of 13 Platoon, Royal Dublin Fusiliers,
being inspected prior to leaving the Royal Barracks.

Royal Dublin Fusiliers setting off on their march through
Dublin on their way to England, 30 April 1915.

there laid out', and they tried to ensure they got issued with
a shovel, much easier to work with than the alternative, a
pick.[29] No trace of their efforts remains today: Flanagan's
Quarry, and the land around it where they must have dug
the trenches, turns out to have been in Clondalkin, adjacent
to today's N7/N50 Red Cow interchange. Now it is all built
over.[30]

When they were not trench-digging, 'D' company were
busy with route marches, rifle practice, and night operations.
'The most ambitious of the last was an occasion on which
the battalion left barracks at 11pm, marched twelve or fifteen
miles into the Dublin mountains, spent the night in the snow
there, and engaged in a sham battle next morning before
marching back.' 'Rifle practice', by contrast, 'was looked on

as something of a holiday, as we went down by train and had nothing to do between our turns of firing except keep ourselves warm'.[31]

But the big advantage of being in Dublin, especially for those in 'D' Company who lived there, was that daily passes were issued. On most days this allowed Fred and his colleagues to be away from the barracks between 4.00 pm and midnight.[32] It must have meant that he was able to see a lot more of Alice than when he had been at the Curragh. They would both have appreciated the gift of 'a few house plants' from the Botanic Gardens – recorded in its donations book in March 1915 – as they did their best to settle into their new home.

'D' Company spent three months in Dublin before departing for England on 30 April. Crowds lined the route as they marched, with bayonets fixed, from the Royal Barracks to North Wall, and thence by ship to Holyhead. *The Irish Times*, reporting on their departure, made much of the social composition of the battalion, and considered that the 'continuous cheering by dense lines of spectators . . . proved that the city pulsates with ardent enthusiasm for the cause of the Allies'.[33]

Not everybody, it would become clear, saw things this way.

Fred and Alice together in England, 1915.

8

Gallipoli

Their immediate destination, it turned out, was Basingstoke, in the south of England, where they joined a number of other regiments and battalions being brought together to form the 10th Irish Division. They were part of a larger force that was to be sent to Gallipoli, in the eastern Mediterranean, reinforcements for the British, Australian and New Zealand troops who were struggling to gain a foothold in the peninsula. The original scheme was conceived by Winston Churchill, then First Lord of the Admiralty, with the aim of opening a new front against the Germans and their Turkish allies. Instead of a swift victory, however, the British force that landed at Gallipoli met fierce resistance from Turkish forces and their offensive soon ground to a halt. Reinforcements would be needed to break the deadlock.

Fred and his colleagues in 'D' company, Royal Dublin Fusiliers, lived in tents outside Basingstoke for nearly three months. 'Not a bad place but very quiet,' was the initial comment on their new home by Private Henry Kavanagh, a solicitor's clerk in civilian life. That perception would soon change. Frank Laird reckoned, after they had been there a while longer, that 'never in their lives did they work so hard'.[1] This was largely down to Sgt-Major William Kee,

Soldiers of the 10th (Irish) Division attending a religious service at their training camp near Basingstoke, Hampshire. In the background are the tents where they lived for three months.

until recently a divinity student at Trinity College, 'who worked us unmercifully until we had the best platoon in the company'.[2] There were more route marches with full equipment, rifle and bayonet training, trench digging, and they engaged in manoeuvres and mock battles with other regiments. The King and Queen came to inspect them, as did Lord Kitchener, Secretary of State for War.

They did get some time off. Fred explored the local flora, found some (carnivorous) sundew plants and sent specimens back to Glasnevin.[3] When he had some leave he must also have visited his home town of Loughborough, for a photograph of him, in uniform, was taken by a local photographer, F. Newton Nield. Mr Nield's studio was at No. 14 High Street, where his family's pharmacy once was.[4]

Another time Alice came to visit, a moment captured in a photograph, marked 'Basingstoke, June 1915', showing her,

Fred, and two of his colleagues from 'D' company, outside in a garden. All three men are in uniform. Frank Laird is sitting on the chair, next to Alice. Standing behind him, pipe in hand, with one arm around Frank's neck, is Cecil Gunning, The camaraderie is plain to see. The scene captured in the photograph, and the happy time they all look to be having, is entirely consistent with Cecil's later observation that Fred's 'wife was very popular with us'.[5] His younger brother Frank was most likely the one who took the photograph.

Studio portrait by F. Newton Neild, Loughborough, 1915.

It was not all jollity, however. Frank also remembered Fred saying, during their time in Basingstoke, that he did not think he 'would live to be very old'.[6] Whether he had in mind his father's, or his brother's, early deaths, or the unknown perils that lay before them, he did not say.

For weeks Fred and his colleagues remained in the dark as to their ultimate destination. But the arrival of khaki drill and

Alice, Fred and fellow soldiers from 'D' Company, Royal Dublin Fusiliers, Basingstoke, 1915.

Comrades-in-arms:
Cecil Gunning,
Frank Gunning and
Guy Cranwill.

pith helmets in the middle of June told them what they were all desperate to know. On 9 July, along with the Sixth Dublins, they departed by train for Devonport and thence to the eastern Mediterranean in the troopship *Alaunia*. After calling in at Gibraltar, Malta and then Alexandria, where they were allowed to go ashore, they arrived at the island of Lemnos, a large naval base, before finally disembarking on the island of Lesbos, 120 miles from the entrance to the Dardanelles.

A week later the two Royal Dublin Fusilier battalions, the 6th and 7th, boarded HMS *Fauvette*, a converted store carrier, bound for Suvla Bay. Frank Gunning complained bitterly that 'D' company were allocated 'a rotten part of the ship, a large empty coal cellar which filled the bow of the boat', so decided to go and sleep on deck under the lifeboats instead. He was joined there by Cecil, Fred and Guy Cranwill ('Molly' as they called him), another friend in No. 2 section.[7]

Fred and Frank Laird, meanwhile, agreed that they would do their utmost to stick together once they arrived.[8]

Suvla Bay was on the western side of the Gallipoli peninsula, to the north of the original landings. The plan was

*Soldiers of 13 platoon, 7th battalion RDF at Basingtoke,
shortly before they left for Gallipoli; (below) Lord Kitchener
looks on as the 7th Battalion Royal Dublin Fusiliers march
past before their departure for Gallipoli.*

to land troops there, attack and occupy Turkish positions on
the surrounding hills, and then cross the peninsula to relieve
pressure on the embattled allied positions to the south. Caught
in a pincer movement the Turkish forces, so it was hoped,
would be either destroyed or forced to surrender, enabling
the navy to sail through the unprotected Dardanelles and
towards Constantinople.

Things went badly wrong from the beginning. The
overall planning and management of the campaign was
abysmal. There were no proper maps; the vital matter of

Guinness Grenadiers: Clarence Fisher, Victor Jeffreson, and Connolly Norman, 13 platoon, RDF. All worked at the Guinness brewery before enlisting.

providing a sufficient supply of water for the men was not attended to; the 7th Battalion's artillery had gone astray and ended up in France, leaving them with no heavy guns; and they were deposited not at their intended landing place but several miles further south. Above all, the general staff had seriously underestimated the strength and determination of the Turkish forces in defending their homeland.

Unlike some of the other battalions, 'D' company was fortunate to avoid casualties from Turkish shelling as they scrambled ashore from the barges that carried them onto the beaches. Fred had a narrow escape, though:

'I was rolled over by a piece [of shrapnel] about spent,' he wrote. 'Luckily I was carrying a sandbag, which the shell hit, and I only got a slight bruise'.[9]

As they moved forward, Frank Gunning remembered, passing 'stretcher-bearers, wounded, dying and dead, and though at first we did not like looking at them, we got used to that also and it didn't bother us'.[10] It was a baptism of fire: 'shells dropping in the water, boats and

HMS Fauvette, *the converted store carrier which took 6th and 7th Battalions, Royal Dublin Fusiliers to Suvla Bay.*

pinnaces trying to tug loads of wounded, the strand littered with casualties and more shells dropping in the long grass of the sand dunes behind, men groaning, and the RAMC working and bandaging like fury.'

The objective for the 7th Dublins was to capture Yilgin Burnu, known to them as 'Chocolate Hill' because of the colour of the burnt earth on its slopes, the result of recent scrub fires. To get there, because they had landed on the wrong beach, they had to undertake a dangerous journey. The first part of it, northwards along the shoreline, was heavy going but there was some cover until they reached the point where the outlet from the dried-up salt lake inland led into the sea. Turkish gunners from the surrounding hills had the spot in their sights and shelled it constantly, but with no alternative route available the Dublins simply had to take their chances. They managed to get across the soft sand and mud without mishap, meeting up with some Inniskilling

Fusiliers on the other side, 'hundreds of men packed under the shelter of the cliffs waiting for the next move forward'.

Others who came after them were not so fortunate and there were numerous casualties. This part of the route consequently came to be known variously as 'Shrapnel Gully' (Frank Gunning) and 'Dunphy's Corner', 'after the place of that name', Frank Laird

(left) Map of the eastern Mediterranean, showing Gallipoli and Suvla Bay. (below) Detailed map of Suvla Bay, showing the location of Salt Lake and Chocolate Hill.

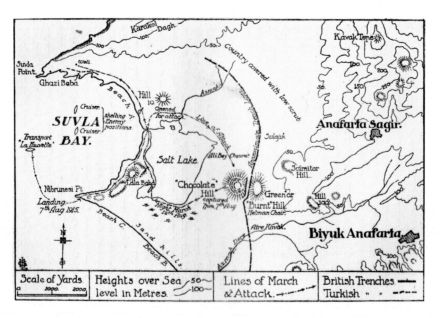

explained, 'where the many funerals, of old and young, pass on their way to Glasnevin', Dublin's well known cemetery.'' Fred would have been more familiar with this than most given his place of work.

Then 'D' company had to turn due east, along the exposed northern perimeter of the salt lake, an even easier target for Turkish guns, and they suffered some casualties. 'Shells were falling everywhere', Frank Gunning remembered. 'Soon we were under rifle fire as well, so we opened out into open order at about ten paces intervals'. His colleagues in No. 2 section nevertheless reached the foot of Chocolate Hill without suffering any casualties, 'running from ditch to ditch over open country' as Frank Laird recalled. In accordance with their agreement, Frank and Fred 'and a few other chaps of our section' managed to stick together for the whole of that

The dried-up salt lake inland from Suvla Bay which 'D' Company had to cross in order to launch their assault on Chocolate Hill, seen here in the background. Painting by Norman Wilkinson.

*British soldiers at an ambulance station on the slopes
of Chocolate Hill, Suvla Bay, 1915.*

day, and 'for most of the time we knew and saw little outside
our small fellowship'.

'We dived into our ditch together when the section leader
gave the order, and rose and rushed on when he gave it again.
We tried to recollect our home training, and to resist the
impulse to crowd together in the safer looking spots, or to
make for the false security of trees or outstanding bushes.
Occasionally one of us tripped and fell on the sun-baked
earth, but immediately relieved the feelings of friends by
jumping up and running on.'[12]

A combined force of Inniskilling, Irish and Dublin
Fusiliers then attacked the Turkish positions on Chocolate
Hill, in the end driving their occupants from their trenches.
But it was a success achieved at heavy cost. There were over
a hundred casualties, 22 of them from 'D' Company.

One of the wounded in 'D' Company was 22-year old Private Hugh Anderson, from Donegal, a civil servant before he enlisted in the Fusiliers. After nightfall he wandered around the trenches, obviously distressed and disoriented, trying to talk to his colleagues. He had gunshot wounds to his arm and his chest, and had a bullet in his stomach. Colleagues bound up his wounds to make him as comfortable as they could, believing he could not have long to live. One of them then volunteered, as Frank Laird recalled, 'to take him to some stretcher bearers and set off in the dark to find them.' Successful in this, the stretcher-bearers carried Anderson down to the beach where he received the medical attention he needed and 'lived to fight another day'.[13]

Members of 'D' Company, RDF, occupying trenches at Chocolate Hill, August 1915. Painting (from a photograph) by Lt. Drummond Fish.

Private Hugh Anderson, 'D' Company, Royal Dublin Fusiliers, wounded in the assault on Chocolate Hill.

Cecil Gunning remembered things a bit differently. In his account it was Fred who volunteered that night to take Anderson to safety, and he recalled seeing the 'two brave fellows' starting off together in the darkness. After a while, though, when Anderson 'became completely exhausted', Fred 'carried him until he got hold of a doctor who gave Andy a morphia pill to ease the pain'. The next morning, having arrived at the beach, Fred saw him safely onto a pinnace which took him to one of the hospital ships, and in the evening made his way back to Chocolate Hill – waiting until it was dark so as to avoid snipers as he crossed the salt lake.[14]

It was, if Cecil Gunning's version of events is accurate, a notable act of bravery and stamina on Fred's part. Young Private Anderson, amazingly, survived his injuries. 'Dangerously ill', he was evacuated to Alexandria, in Egypt, and treated in hospital for his wounds; he recovered and was invalided out of the army seven weeks later. In February 1916, back in uniform again, he was attached to the 10th battalion, Royal Dublin Fusiliers, promoted to sergeant and then commissioned as a lieutenant, joining the 16th Irish division on the western front. After the war he returned to the civil service, rising eventually to the rank of Permanent Secretary. He was very fortunate to have survived.[15]

On Monday 9 August, the day after Fred returned to Chocolate Hill, 'D' company advanced further inland from their trenches but were met with fierce enemy fire. Frank Laird was wounded in the shoulder, stretchered back to the beaches and evacuated to Lemnos – distinctly relieved, he wrote later, to have 'found himself alive and out of the hell of Gallipoli'.[16] Before he was taken away he asked a colleague 'to take my glasses to my friend Ball from whom I had been separated that moment for the first time'.[17]

The remainder of 'D' company were forced back to their trenches and stayed put for the next few days, plagued in the searing heat by thirst, lice and swarms of flies (a 'dreadful pest' Frank Gunning said, and 'no wonder there was such a lot of dysentery').[18] There were further casualties from shelling, among them Sgt Sutcliffe, who was badly wounded in the leg by shrapnel while directing trench digging. Connolly Norman, promoted to lance-corporal, took his place as section leader.

The decision by the generals not to advance on the first day, when they had the chance to do so, proved to be one of the many grave errors of the campaign. Had they done so, many believed, they could have captured the hills beyond while the Turks were still in retreat. But the opportunity was missed and reinforcements, well equipped with machine-guns and grenades, were rushed in, enabling the Turkish forces to halt the belated Irish advance in its tracks. On 12 August the 7th Dublins were relieved by another regiment and made their way back to Lala Baba, the base camp close to the beach, rejoining the rest of the 10th division. Frank Gunning, like the others, 'was absolutely dead with fatigue', but having been separated from the rest of No. 2 section, was relieved to be able to rejoin them once they got there.

They had little respite. Several days later the Fusiliers were involved in a second assault, this time up the slopes of Kiretch Tepe to the north, in support of the 6th Dublins and 7th Munster Fusiliers who had taken the narrow ridge. On the night of the 15th August, and the following morning, 'D' company was involved in desperate fighting amidst the boulders on the hillside, losing many men to hand grenades lobbed onto their positions by Turkish soldiers. They had none to hurl back, save those they could catch before they exploded, and they found that rifles were useless in this situation. Private Wilkin, famously, caught five grenades and hurled them back before the sixth exploded and killed him. Others retaliated by simply hurling back stones. In the end they launched a bayonet charge. They made some ground, held the line but suffered severe losses.

'Every wave of our men that went over that ridge never came back' Cecil Gunning wrote later. 'It was hell let loose'. He and his brother Frank, with the rest of No. 2 section, were about to join a second bayonet charge when at the very last moment the order came from a staff officer to hold back and retire to the trenches, already full of dead and wounded. Both were convinced that this last-minute change of plan had saved their lives. It would have been 'pure suicide' to have gone ahead, Cecil said, as there was 'an absolute wall of bullets coming over the ridge'. Their relief at this narrow escape was 'indescribable'.[19]

But overall it was a disaster. By the time 'D' Company was relieved on the morning of 16 August they had lost 11 officers, 54 men killed or wounded, and 15 were missing – leaving them with less than half their original strength. Not a single officer was left standing.[20] Fred and the two Gunnings were lucky to have escaped with their lives. Victor Jeffreson,

'On the way to "The Pimple"': the 7th Battalion, RDF, make their way
towards Kiretch Tepe for the engagement of 15 and 16 August;
(below) 'In the trenches, Karakol Dagh': the 7th battalion dig in
on the lower slopes of Kiretch Tepe.

formerly a clerk at the Guinness brewery, was another in No. 2 section who survived the debacle – only to be killed a few days later.[21] That evening the Turks re-took the ridge.

Ironically, despite the devastating losses, the British assault may have come closer to success than they realised. After the war the German commander at Gallipoli, Liman von Sanders, wrote in his memoirs that the battle for the summit of Kiretch Tepe was a close run thing, and that if the British had prevailed 'success might have attended their operations as a whole'. From its commanding position over the Suvla plains below, he believed, 'a decisive attack could have been made'.[22] Only, however, if the summit had been taken.

The remnants of 'D' company were then moved to Scimitar Hill, about a mile and a half to the east of Chocolate Hill. After participating in an unsuccessful attack on Turkish positions on 21 August, they dug in, occupying trenches facing opposite their Turkish counterparts. The situation thereafter became one of stalemate, resembling that on the western front, with neither side being able to overcome the other. Most could now see that there was no longer any prospect of victory.

This is also the point at which we hear Fred's own voice, thanks to the survival of a letter he wrote to Sir Frederick Moore at the end of August. He was keen to make light of their situation. Physical conditions, he told Sir Frederick, were his main preoccupation, and there was no mention of the horrors he and his colleagues had gone through. Sand got into everything but he was pleased to say he remained 'fit and well . . . A touch of rheumatism in my knee has been my worst trouble', the consequence of cold nights he thought. He went on:

'The worst of it is in a front trench, one gets very little sleep at night with guard now and again, trench-digging and fatigues. Last night I was on a covering party towards the enemy's trenches during an attack, and we had a warm time. There's continued sniping going on all the time: one of our men was hit just now in the leg while out gathering sticks for a fire. We have to do our own cooking and make tea in this trench. We are regaled with the interesting sight of the naval guns sending shells on the mountain held by the enemy, but their guns are cleverly concealed and the country is very difficult in front. Aeroplanes pass over, and we saw a fight between a Taube and one of ours, but no result.'

News from home was slow to reach them. 'Seven weeks after leaving England we got our first post, but now it is coming more regularly. Yesterday I received Irish Gardening among some other papers sent by my wife, and

The lower slopes of Scimitar Hill, showing British warships offshore in the distance.

it is a very interesting number.' Edited by John Besant in Fred's absence, it must have come as a welcome distraction from the hardships of life in the trenches. So were the plants and flowers he saw around him, which he knew Sir Frederick would want to know about too. Acres of *Juncus acutus* (a sharp-pointed rush) 'gave us a rest and some shelter from rifle- and machine-gun fire', and he spoke of the 'dense scrub' covering the ground, 'consisting mostly of *Quercus coccifera* [Kermes oak], I believe'. There were also some good-sized trees of various kinds, 'such as willow, Lombardy and white poplars, olive, Pyrus, Ulmus [elm], and an oak which I am not sure, and enclose a leaf, also seed of a Hypericum [St. John's wort]'.

Fred regretted missing what must have been the glorious sight of 'Cistus [rock rose] on some of the mountains' since their flowers were now over, but he had already sent Sir Frederick seeds of two species, part of a consignment he had managed to send 'by Lacey some time ago'.

This was William Lacey, the caretaker at the Royal Botanic Gardens, who was also, Fred assured Sir Frederick, 'fit and well' when he last saw him. He was part of the 5th battalion, Royal Irish Fusiliers, which was sent to Gallipoli and then participated – alongside the Royal Dublin Fusiliers – in the assault on Chocolate Hill. So perhaps their conversation about sending seeds back to Glasnevin took place in the trenches they occupied after capturing them from the Turks. Lacey was now regimental sergeant-major, the most senior of the non-commissioned officers, so should have been well placed to help Fred with his request. Their consignment did not take long to reach Dublin: five packets of 'seeds of various plants' from 'Mr Ball, Dardanelles', were recorded in the Botanic Gardens' accessions book for August 1915.[23]

Sgt-Major Lacey, it might be added, survived both Gallipoli and subsequent postings in Salonika and Egypt, returning to his old job at Glasnevin after being demobilised in 1919.[24]

As well as writing to 'the boss', Fred also kept a diary, three days of which were reproduced subsequently in *Irish Gardening*. From their quite personal tone his entries look as though he had Alice in mind as he wrote them, an opportunity perhaps to reassure her in the face of the desperately worrying news in the

Sgt.-Major William Lacey, Royal Irish Fusiliers, Anglo-Boer War veteran and caretaker at the Botanic Gardens, Glasnevin.

Dublin newspapers of the heavy casualties being suffered in Gallipoli. He probably envisaged this diary being shared with his mother and others in his family.

Here is part of his entry for 27 August. 'Perhaps you would like to know what life in a trench is like,' he began, echoing his words to Alice when he told her of his daily routine at the Curragh nine months before. 'The sides of the trench are undercut in places like little caves, in these we sleep at intervals, but we are too crowded to have one each. At night we are on guard for three separate hours; sometimes have a turn at trench-digging and carrying food, both day and night, and are awakened at 4.30 or 5.00 am: besides sometimes there are false alarms, so usually one's rest is broken, so we make it up in the day if not in fatigues. On first arriving our food consisted of biscuit and bully beef, but it has gradually improved, and we now get jam, bacon, rice, potatoes, tea,

British troops in trenches on Chocolate Hill.

sugar and condensed milk, and to our great joy this morning half a loaf of bread was served out to each man. The nights are very cold, but the days extremely hot and sunny. This is the sixth day we have had in this trench, but it is not too bad at all.'

Two days later, on 29 August, a Sunday, Fred volunteered with several others to go and fetch the post. Instead of getting it from the usual place they found they had to go all the way to the beach, four miles away, to collect it. It was heavy going as they had to walk through loose sand bordering the sea and along the salt lake, a dangerous route and still within range of Turkish artillery. But they made it safely and Fred had a dip in the sea, 'the first wash I had for over a week!'

As before, his attention was drawn to the flowers he found along the way. 'I came across a pretty lot of maidenhair fern this morning growing near a spring,' and then a 'tiny love-in-a mist' growing wild, along with 'olives, brooms, sea lavender, sea holly, and many other interesting plants.' The sight of them prompted some further reflections. 'A knowledge of plants and botany always makes a walk interesting, and conveys much useful information. Plants have their tastes as well as we have. By the plants growing on land we can usually tell whether it is chalky or sandy, or if it is salt marsh at any time of the year and partly covered by sea; also, to a certain extent, the altitude of the land, and so on.' This was the physical and mental world in which Fred wished to remain.

Fred and his company remained in the trenches until early September, suffering further casualties from illness, shell shrapnel, snipers' bullets and illness. Dysentery was the worst of the illnesses, claiming, among others, Frank Gunning, who had to be evacuated to Lemnos a couple of weeks earlier. Fred, it seems, was afflicted too, but he carried on. As it grew colder, especially at nights, frostbite became an additional hazard. Some protection, though, was provided by a stray Post Office mailbag used to deliver mail which nobody had claimed. Fred and Cecil Gunning requisitioned it and used it as a sleeping bag. 'It came almost up to our chests and it kept our legs and feet beautifully warm'.[25]

A few days later, on 9 September, 'D' company was relieved of trench duty and withdrew to a supposed 'rest camp' at Lala Baba, away from the front line. The description was widely derided since the low hills of Lala Baba were within range of Turkish artillery and 'the rest bivouacs on the beach' provided scant protection for anybody.[26] In a letter back home Paddy Tobin, an officer in 'D' Company, said he thought being at the 'rest camp' meant 'remaining on the beach and getting shelled'. By the time his company was back at Lala Baba he was dead, one of the many killed in the action at Kiretch Tepe.[27]

'During the four days they were here (until the 13th)', it was reported of their stay at the 'rest camp', 'D' Company was 'subjected to continual shell-fire', suffering numerous casualties.[28] On the last day the shelling was more intense, and more lethal, than ever. In the words of the regimental staff diary, 'Heavy shellfire caused casualties: medical officer wounded; other ranks, 5 killed, 20 wounded.'

'Other ranks', as was the custom, were not usually mentioned by name. Fred was one of the '5 killed'.

Frank Laird heard what happened from his former colleagues when he was in hospital recovering from his injuries: 'While waiting on the beach with other sick (he was ill with dysentery) a shell fell near him, and wounded one of his comrades. True to his nature he waited to help the wounded man instead of rushing for cover. A second shell followed the first and he was struck in the back.' He was taken to the 31st Field Ambulance station nearby, but the medics could not save him. 'In his weak condition,' Laird wrote, 'he had not vitality to make a fight for life and he died some hours later.'[29]

Cecil's reaction, when he heard the news of Fred's death, was to throw away the old mail bag 'in disgust', unwilling to use it once his friend was no longer there to share it.[30]

His account of what had happened was briefer, and perhaps not strictly accurate, but it captured another truth. Fred, he said, 'was picking flowers to send home when a shell killed him instantly.' His description echoes the

A view of Suvla Bay from the top of the hill known as Lala Baba.
Fred lost his life on the beach below. Painting by Lt Drummond Fish.

report of another friend whose last memory was of seeing Fred 'lying behind a big boulder digging up "weeds" with Turkish bullets spitting around him too'.[31] Both expressed the poignancy of the contrast between the actions of a man of peace, fascinated by plants and flowers even in the midst of war, and his violent end.

Canon Maclean, the Anglican chaplain, formerly rector of Rathkeale, County Limerick, officiated at Fred's burial in the makeshift cemetery close by.[32]

Two weeks later, on 29 September, what remained of 'D' company were evacuated to Lemnos, and then departed to Macedonia for a new campaign. In mid-December, once it had become clear that the situation was hopeless, the evacuation began of the entire allied expeditionary force – over 250,000 men – from the Gallipoli peninsula. It was one of the few operations of the campaign that was successfully accomplished. From the British, and Irish, perspective it had been an unmitigated disaster, with nearly 50,000 lives lost. Only 79 of the original 286 in 'D' Company, Royal Dublin Fusiliers, were evacuated from Gallipoli: 37 had been killed, the remainder had been wounded or were ill, mostly suffering from dysentery. In 13 platoon, 25 men were evacuated from an original strength of 60.[33]

Of the four friends in No. 2 section who gathered in that garden in Basingstoke in June before they left for Gallipoli, only Cecil Gunning came through unscathed: Frank Laird was in hospital recovering from his wounds, Frank Gunning was in Lemnos with dysentery, and Fred was dead. Frank Gunning, once he had recovered, would join the Inniskilling Fusiliers, only to be killed on the Somme in July 1916.

Quercus coccifera, *Kermes oak, common on the Gallipoli peninsula. Fred collected its acorns and sent them back to Glasnevin.*

Back home, Dublin was aghast as news of the tragedy at Gallipoli unfolded, and the newspapers carried growing lists of casualties. For the wives and families of soldiers serving in the Royal Dublin Fusiliers and the other Irish regiments it was an agonizing time, waiting and hoping. For some, like Alice, whose story we will return to, there was the worst imaginable outcome. Around her, and across Ireland, grief and sadness gave way to anger at the pointless sacrifice of young lives – made worse by the failure of the generals to recognise publicly the full extent of the Irish contribution.[34]

Memorial at St. Mobhi's church in Glasnevin.

9

Memories and Memorials

Fred's death was announced in *The Irish Times* on 2 October and the *Irish Independent* two days later. *The Times* called him 'one of the best known botanists and horticulturalists in Ireland', and 'keenly devoted to his profession... Quite recently,' it added, 'the collection at the Royal Botanical Gardens were enriched by a consignment of plants which he sent home from the Dardanelles to Sir F. W. Moore.' 'Numerous seedlings,' John Besant confirmed later, would grow from seeds he had sent.[1]

More detailed obituaries followed over the next weeks and months. Herbert Cowley, wounded on the western front but now back at work as editor of *The Garden*, spoke of 'a life full of promise and still in the vigour of youth [being] given for his country and the cause of justice'. He recalled their trip to Bulgaria and remembered Fred as 'a delightful companion, unassuming, sincere, and a most lovable man'.[2]

John Besant wrote in similar vein in the *Kew Guild Journal* and said that his death 'comes as a great shock to everyone at Glasnevin . . . In his position as Assistant to the Keeper he came into contact, more or less, with every member of the staff, and was universally liked and respected. His unfailing courtesy endeared him to everyone, and a large circle of friends in Ireland mourn his loss and will not forget him.'[3]

The longest obituary was written by Sir Frederick Moore for *Irish Gardening*. It recounted the details of his life, his achievements in the field of horticulture, his 'quiet, gentle manner' and 'open-handed generosity', and also his selfless bravery in Gallipoli. 'Letters from soldiers in the same detachment received since his death give instances of bravery and self-sacrifice unostentatiously performed, and of which no hint is given in his letters.' One of these letters, probably from Frank Laird, recalled his 'soft voice, kind brown eyes, chuckling laugh and yet deep and powerful nature'.[4]

Dublin's wider scientific community mourned his passing too. On behalf of the Dublin Naturalists' Field Club, J. de W. Hinch wrote to Alice to convey his condolences and 'to place on record their sense of the great loss to botanical sciences in Ireland'. A similar letter came from the Dublin Microscopical Club, 'stating with what very sincere feelings of sympathy the news of Mr Ball's tragic end had been received by the members of the club, and to state how highly he was esteemed by all of us'.[5]

Quite how Alice coped can only be imagined. Instead of the prospect of welcoming Fred home there were the grim rituals that came with news of his death, the return of his few possessions, the award of a war gratuity and a meagre widow's pension. Perhaps the knowledge that Fred was so loved and admired, as the letters and obituaries make clear, brought some solace. Perhaps the poem that Alice pasted into her scrapbook, next to these obituaries, offered some comfort too. It is entitled 'Gallipoli' and is by Lance-Corporal Eugene Duffy, Fred's comrade-in-arms and fellow horticulturist (see Appendix). He describes the voyage to Suvla Bay, the feelings of the men as they approach the shore, their bravery in the face of shelling that burst around them, the casualties they suffered. The poem ends with his tribute to a feat of arms that 'gives added lustre to our deathless heritage', and the glory and honour of 'unselfish, noble deeds, /And young lives bravely sacrificed when King and Country needs'.[6]

* * *

When the war ended Fred's death was remembered anew, his memory enshrined in war memorials in Turkey, England and Ireland. He is buried at the Lala Baba cemetery close to where he fell, his grave placed with 215 others. His headstone carries the words 'Greater love hath no man than this', chosen by Alice and added in 1923, eight years after his death.[7] His name is also on war memorials at Kew Gardens, in his home town of Loughborough, at the Freemasons' Hall in Dublin, and at St Mobhi's parish church, Glasnevin, a few hundred yards from their last home.[8]

The Lala Baba cemetery, Suvla Bay.

*The headstone over Fred's grave. It records his age as 36
but he was a month short of his 36th birthday when he died.*

But memories of Fred's life and work lived on too, not just
of his death. At Glasnevin the plants he loved were a daily
reminder to his colleagues of what had inspired him. Among
them were the *Haberlea* he brought back from Bulgaria, the
memory of which, he once said, would always be with him.
John Besant called it 'a wonderful collection', 'the finest
display of *haberleas* to be seen in cultivation anywhere',
and that it increased in beauty as each year passed.[9] Fred's
Escallonia hybrids lived on too, most notably *Escallonia* 'C.F.
Ball', with its deep red flowers, named only after his death,
and then cultivated at Glasnevin, Daisy Hill, the Donard
nursery and elsewhere. It proved to be a commercial as well
as an aesthetic success, available in nurseries and grown in
gardens to this day. One of them, planted in 2016, adorns
the National War Memorial Gardens at Islandbridge,
Dublin.[10] Another stands alongside *Escallonia* 'Alice' in

front of the Great Palm House at today's National Botanic Gardens in Glasnevin.

There was another memorial to Fred Ball, perhaps the most poignant of all. Among the seeds he sent back from Gallipoli were acorns from *Quercus coccifera*, Kermes oak, the shrub-like evergreen which was common on the peninsula. Some of these went to his friend George Smith in Newry and at least one grew into a healthy plant on the slopes of the Daisy Hill Nursery. Over twenty years later, his health failing, and

Memorials in Ireland and England –
at the Freemasons' Hall in Dublin (right)
and Loughborough Grammar School (below).

with nobody to leave his business to, George Smith began to auction off his stock, preparing for its closure.[11]

Before this took place he wanted to find a good home for Fred's *Quercus coccifera*, given its association with a man he described as a 'dear friend' and 'one of Nature's gentlemen'.[12] Early in 1937, therefore, he offered it to Commander Frank Gilliland, a friend and regular customer of his, who owned the Brook Hall Estate, just outside Derry in Northern Ireland. Gilliland, he knew, would appreciate it, not just because he had a passion for rare trees, and had planted a much-admired arboretum, but because his own cousin, Lt. Billy Gilliland, Royal Inniskilling Fusiliers, had died at Gallipoli too. The tree could thus serve as a fitting memorial to both men. And George Smith could feel he had secured the future of a tree he had tended for over twenty years.[13]

Frank Gilliland was pleased to accept it. On 10 April 1937 the *Londonderry Sentinel*, under the headline 'Oak with unique

Lt. Billy Gilliland.

history', reported that it had become 'the latest addition to the extensive collection of shrubs at Brook Hall, Londonderry.' An entry in his journal the following year, in August 1938, records that the *Quercus coccifera* was planted on his estate with a view of 'lily pond, flagstaff and river', and that it was 'given by G. N. Smith to me, from an acorn sent to him from Gallipoli by C. F. Ball,

The view from the garden at Brook Hall, looking out over the
River Foyle, from the spot where Fred's Gallipoli oak once grew.

Royal Dublin Fusiliers, who was killed in action before the
acorn reached Ireland'.[14]

Perhaps it could be seen as more than just a reminder of
two young lives lost on distant shores. Gallipoli has never had
the symbolic significance for Ireland as it has for Australia
and New Zealand, new nations in the making. Ireland may
have been on this threshold too but its subsequent history
ensured that it was the 1916 Easter Rising that resonated most
powerfully, and that the experiences of the tens of thousands
of Irishmen who fought for the British cause during the First
World War were long overlooked.

But things have changed. Ireland's historical memory
has broadened to encompass the sacrifices of Gallipoli, the
Somme, and other battlefields where Irish lives were lost. It
can surely find a space too for the modest young Englishman

who made his name at one of Ireland's foremost national institutions, made his home in Dublin, and then – when the moment came – chose to join Dublin's regiment, the Royal Dublin Fusiliers.

Fred Ball's *Quercus coccifera*, the Gallipoli oak that once grew at Daisy Hill and Brook Hall, has not survived. That is no reason, however, why an acorn cannot be planted anew to honour Fred's memory, and that of the others who died with him at Gallipoli – wherever they came from. Just as Gallipoli oaks grown from acorns sent back by ANZAC soldiers honour them to this day in Australia – a living connection with a painful but formative episode in the country's history.[15]

* * *

Fred's life and the manner of his death raise broader issues of historical memory but they had deeply personal consequences as well, particularly for Alice. No letters of hers have survived to suggest how she coped with her loss. We know that she stayed on at their new house in Ballymun Road, and was involved, according to one report, in the work of the comforts committee, providing 'cheer and help to the wounded'.[16] She became close to May Laird, Frank Laird's wife, and on at least one occasion went to stay with her at her family home in Sandycove.[17] May was a wartime bride like her, engaged to Frank before he was sent to Gallipoli and married to him when he returned. She would have been better able than most to understand what Alice had gone through.

Alice suffered another loss with the sudden death of her sister Emily in 1917. Emily's husband had abandoned her and their three young children several years earlier, taking himself off to Canada. After Emily died the children were cared for by the Church of Ireland orphanage in Clyde Road, Ballsbridge. Alice was a regular visitor and kept a close eye on their welfare.

As time passed she set about rebuilding a life on her own. In 1918 she learnt to drive, not at that time a common thing for women to do, acquiring a certificate that said she had 'completed a full course of motor-driving and mechanism', and 'thoroughly understands running repairs'.[18] A few weeks before the end of the war she joined the newly formed Women's Royal Air Force as a driver, based at Tallaght, remaining there until she was demobilised in September 1919. Her work, according to her certificate of discharge, was 'very satisfactory', she was 'a most efficient and careful

Alice (centre) and fellow drivers, WRAF, Tallaght aerodrome, 1918/19.

Group portrait, WRAF, Tallaght, 1918/19. Alice is possibly the fourth from left, back row.

driver', and her personal character 'exemplary'. The senior WRAF officer who vouched for her, it is interesting to note, was Marjorie Scholefield, daughter of her family's solicitor.[19]

It must have been around this time that she met my

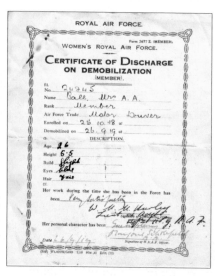

Alice's Certificate on Demobilization from the WRAF, 26 September 1919.

grandfather, Robert ('Bob') Kinghan. He was one of the sons of a Church of Ireland clergyman from Swinford, County Mayo, whose family came to live in Dublin after he died in 1908. A student at Trinity College when war broke out, Robert was also an instructor in the Officers' Training Corps – and remembered as such, by coincidence, by Frank Laird when he returned to the college for military training in the autumn of 1914.[20] Robert Kinghan joined the Royal Irish Fusiliers, served with them on the western front, was wounded three times, awarded the Military Cross and ended up with the rank of major. But his family experienced wartime tragedy too: Robert's younger brother Albert, also in the Royal Irish Fusiliers, was killed at the Somme in October 1916.

Robert stayed on in the army after the war only to find himself caught up in another – the Irish War of Independence. Transferred to the South Lancashire regiment, part of

Major R.W. Kinghan, MC, Royal Irish Fusiliers, who Alice married in 1922.

the 24th Brigade, he was stationed at the Royal Barracks in Dublin at a time when hostilities were intensifying in the city and the country as a whole. For much of his time there he was confined to barracks because of the danger of ambush and assassination. It can't have made courting Alice easy. 'We' re not allowed out at all in the ordinary way,' he told her on 24 November 1920, three days after Bloody Sunday, but added that 'I occasionally see the town by darting out in an armoured car for recreation and to get away from the office'.[21] He must have taken part in military operations too for later in life he would regale his family with tales of trying to track down Michael Collins, the IRA's Director of Intelligence, but always in vain.

In 1921 Robert resigned his commission and was married to Alice in London early in 1922. Many in Ireland's Anglo-Irish community, especially those with military connections, moved to England rather than contemplate the uncertainties of the new Irish Free State. In their case, though, it seems that limited employment opportunities in Ireland, and the disapproval of Robert's family of his marriage to Alice, were more important in their decision.[22]

Alice took Fred's memory with her. While embracing her new life, and soon with children of her own to care for – my mother Patricia was born in 1923 – she kept in touch with Fred's mother Mary and his sister Connie. Mary also got to know Eileen, Alice's niece, one of Emily's three children – and my godmother. In 1932, when Alice's own mother died, Mary wrote to offer her condolences, saying how glad she was that Alice had her 'darling children' to enrich her life. They could have been her grandchildren. She signed off her letter, 'Your loving little mother, M.B. Ball'.[23]

Alice and Connie stayed in contact too. Among the family letters I found was one from my mother to her mother and father, when she was nine years old, telling them that 'Aunty Connie sent me 2/6 for my birthday.' So the connection passed on to the next generation.

*　*　*

I knew virtually nothing of Fred Ball until I read his letters to Alice and investigated further. I hope the story of his life, and of his brief time with Alice, will interest others as well. He was, as *The Irish Times* recognised, 'one of the best known botanists and horticulturalists in Ireland', and devoted to his profession. Few would have disagreed with

Frank Laird's prediction that he 'would have gone far in his calling had he not found a glorious end in Gallipoli'.[24]

In truth, as Laird recognised too, he had already gone a long way. Despite being cut off in its prime, his life was one of achievement as well as promise. His legacy lies in his work as Assistant Keeper at the Royal Botanic Gardens in Dublin, as editor of the journal *Irish Gardening*, and in the hybrid plants he created, the *Escallonia* named after him the most notable of them. For seven or eight years he was at the heart of what was, in retrospect, something of a golden age for Irish horticulture, and he made an important contribution to it.

Among those he was close to Fred inspired love and fellowship. Frank Laird believed he was 'a friend on whom one might count for a lifetime'. Alice kept his letters and photographs safe for the rest of her life and treasured his memory. It was his mother Mary, though, who provided the most fitting epitaph. 'Few men,' she wrote, when she sent Fred's photograph to the Imperial War Museum in 1917, 'were better beloved by all who knew him, or gave up happier prospects than he did when he went to the Dardanelles.'[25]

One can only wonder about the life that lay before him had it not ended so tragically.

Appendix

Gallipoli

*By Lance-Corporal Eugene Duffy, 12536, 7th Batt.
Royal Dublin Fusiliers, formerly foreman gardener
to the Earl of Meath at Kilruddery, Bray*

I

Night! And a million stars are shining o'er the deep,
Mirror'd on its bosom, and in the waves that leap
Away from the bows of the vessel, speeding her anxious way,
And eager to reach her ordered place just at the break of day.
The figures swarming on her decks in the warm Eastern night.
So grey and ghost-like they appear under the pale star-light.
No lights are lit; no voices heard; there's need for caution
    when
From stem to stern she carries a thousand fighting men.
Some sit and wonder in their minds of what the dawn will
    bring,
And some just listen to the song the wind and waters sing.
Some lie awake and let their thoughts to loved ones fondly
    roam,
And in uneven, fitful sleep, some hap'ly dream of home.

II

Dawn! O'er the bleak forbidding hills is creep-on apace,
And slowly grim Gallipoli unveils its rugged face.
Our vessel now has reached the place, her task is safely done,
But for her human freight remains a landing to be won.
Ah! Many a soldier lad looks on with hope and courage filled,
Whose gallant heart, e'er dawn again, shall be for ever stilled.
And watch their comrades one by one climb down the
    gangway stair,
To board the squat, black lighter, which takes them over there
To the narrow strip of landing place upon the shingly beach,
That all who look pray silently they may in safety reach.
'Tis not to be! The shrapnel screams, and bursting overhead,
Takes toll from 'mong those gallant lads, of wounded and of
    dead.

III

The landing's made, and on they rush, 'mid storm of shot and
    shell,
And bravely filling up the gaps where'er a comrade fell.
Now, with their feet on Turkish soil, they never will turn back
Until on yonder distant hills they plant the Union Jack.
Our brave Colonial troops are there, so ready, staunch and true,
There, too, the gallant R.N.D, the lads in navy blue.
From England and Old Ireland, from Scotland and from Wales,
Each man resolved to show the world that Britain now prevails.
The history of our race this day is enriched by another page
Of glory, and of honour, and unselfish, noble deeds,
And young lives bravely sacrificed when King and Country
    needs.

Endnotes

Chapter 1: Early Years

1 Kinghan Family Papers, CFB to Alice Lane, 14 March 1913.

2 Death certificate, Alfred Ball; the business was taken over by George J. Baldwin (advertisement in *Loughborough Herald and North Leics Gazette*, 6 September 1889, and 1891 census for 14 High Street, Loughborough).

3 Loughborough Grammar School archives, school register. I am indebted to John Weitzel, Loughborough GS archivist, for making this material available to me and for providing much other information. See www.lgs-heritage.org for more on the school's history.

4 'Old Loughburian killed in the Dardanelles', *Loughborough Echo*, 8 October 1915. This piece is unsigned but from internal evidence looks as if it was written by Fred's mother or draws upon information supplied by her.

5 Kinghan Family Papers, indenture agreement with Charles Frederick Ball, 7 April 1896.

6 Roderick Floud, *An Economic History of the English Garden*, London: Allen Lane, 2019, esp. pp. 163–75 on apprentices and their working conditions. Fred later recalled being reminded – by the gift of some mince pies – 'of the time when I first left home and used to go home for the weekends' (Kinghan Family Papers, CFB to Alice, n.d. [1912]).

7   For William Barron, see Paul Elliott, Charles Watkins and Stephen Daniels, 'William Barron (1805–91) and nineteenth century British arboriculture: Evergreens in Victorian indus-trial-izing society', *Garden History*, vol. 35, supplement: cultural and historical geographies of the arboretum (2007), pp. 129–148.

8   Kew MSS, C. F. Ball staff file, application form, May 1900.

9   Glasnevin MSS 27, testimonials for C.F. Ball from William Barron & Sons and Peter Barr & Sons.

10 On Peter Barr, see Bob Davenport, 'Peter Barr: The "daffodil king",' https://studiedmonuments.wordpress.com/2015/03/11/peter-barr-the-daffodil-king/ accessed 16 August 2020; 'Death of Mr Peter Barr', *The Garden*, 25 Sept 1909, pp. 475-6.

11 'The world of flowers – among the daffodils', *Daily News*, 29 April 1899, quoted in *Barr's Gold Medal Daffodils*, catalogue autumn 1900, p. 2.

12 'Mr P. Rudolph Barr', *The Gardeners' Magazine*, 8 April 1911; 'Workers among the flowers: Peter Rudolph Barr', *The Garden*, 4 December 1909, p. 587.

13 Catalogue, autumn 1900, p. 1.

14 Kew MSS, C.F.Ball staff file, CFB to Royal Botanic Gardens, Kew, 8 May 1900.

15 It was also a requirement that applicants should have been 'employed not less than 5 years in good private gardens or nurseries'. Fred, as he indicated on his application form, had had four and a half years' service, but the shortfall seems to have been overlooked.

16 Kew MSS, C.F. Ball staff file, CFB to Royal Botanic Gardens, Kew, 18 May 1900.

17 Listed as *Mentha arvensis* × *spicata* = *M.gracilis* on the herbaria@home website. Fred's specimen ended up in the herbarium of the Botanic Gardens, Glasnevin, presumably deposited after he went to work there in 1906.

Chapter 2: Training at Kew

1 Donal McCracken, *Gardens of Empire: Botanical Institutions of the Victorian British Empire*, London: Leicester University Press, 1997, p. 78.

2 Ray Desmond and F. Nigel Hepper, *A Century of Kew Plantsmen: A celebration of the Kew Guild*, Richmond: Kew Guild, 1993, p. 141; E.J. Wallis and Herman Spooner, *The Royal Gardens at Kew Illustrated* (second edition, 1908), pp. 51-7; W. Dallimore, 'Chronicle of an old Kewite', *Kew Guild Journal*, 1955, pp. 381-6.

3 Kew MSS, William Dallimore,'Reminiscences', p. 323.

4 Dallimore, 'Reminiscences', p. 416.

5 Dallimore, 'Reminiscences', pp. 416-7.

6 Ray Desmond, *Kew: The History of the Royal Botanic Gardens*, London: Harvill Press with Royal Botanic Gardens, Kew, 1995, esp. pp. 282–5. *Kew Guild Journal*, 1900, p. 6; Dallimore, 'Reminiscences', p. 464.

7 Kew MSS, C.F. Ball staff file. Beatrix Potter, quoted in *Kew: The History of the Botanic Gardens*, p. 285; Glasnevin MSS 27, Watson to Moore, 20 Dept 1906.

8 'Mutual Improvement Society', *Kew Guild Journal*, Dec 1903, p. 117.

9 Dallimore,'Reminiscences', p. 321.

10 *Kew Guild Journal*, December 1903, p. 64.

11 *Kew Guild Journal*, December 1903, p. 115.

12 'In Memoriam: Charles Frederick Ball', by J W B, *Kew Guild Journal*, December 1916, p. 307; 'John William Besant, A.H.R.H.S., F. Inst. P.A.', *Kew Guild Journal*, 1944, p. 217; 'British Botany Club', *Kew Guild Journal*, 1904, p. 174.

13 'Walter Irving', Kew Guild Journal, 1928, p. 301.

14 Glasnevin MSS 27, W. Watson to F.W. Moore, 20 September 1906 (copy). Fred was promoted to sub-foreman on 19 June 1902.

15 Description based on W.J. Bean, *The Royal Botanic Gardens Kew* London: Cassell, 1908, pp. 209-15 and E.J. Wallis and Herman Spooner, *Illustrations of the Royal Botanic Gardens, Kew,* London: Royal Botanic Gardens, Kew, 1908, pp. 34-6.

16 John Campbell left Kew in 1904 to take up a job as Superintendent of Government Gardens and Experimental Plantations in Perak and spent the rest of his career in the far east, *Kew Guild Journal*, September 1931, pp. 75-6.

17 *Sheffield Daily Telegraph*, 25 July 1906; Glasnevin MSS 27, W. Watson to F.W. Moore, 20 September 1906 (copy).

18 Kew MSS, C.F.B Staff file.

19 Glasnevin MSS 27, W. Watson to F. W. Moore, 20 September 1906; E. Charles Nelson and Eileen M. McCracken, *The Brightest Jewel: A History of the National Botanic Gardens, Glasnevin,* Dublin, Kilkenny: Boethius Press, 1987, pp. 205–6.

20 *Brightest Jewel*, p. 207.

21 Glasnevin MSS 27, Moore to H.B. White, Dept. of Agriculture and Technical Instruction, 4 December 1906.

22 Glasnevin MSS 27, Moore to H.B. White, 11 December 1906.

Chapter 3: Assistant Keeper, Royal Botanic Gardens, Glasnevin

1   *Brightest Jewel*, p 188.

2   *Brightest Jewel*, p. 203.

3   Glasnevin MSS 27, Moore to White, 11 January 1907.

4   Kew MSS, DC 131/31-344, no. 130, Moore to Prain, 15 April 1907.

4   RHS Lindley Library, E.A. Bowles papers, EAB 2.6.2.1, Moore to Bowles, 25 March 1907.

5   *Brightest Jewel*, p. 207.

6   *Irish Independent*, 12 March 1909.

7   Glasnevin MSS 27, minute no 150433.

8   'Obituary', *Irish Gardening*, November 1915, p. 161.

9   Kinghan Family Papers, CFB to Alice, 19 March 1913.

10 *Brightest Jewel*, p 209.

11 'Dublin Naturalists' Field Club: November 12, Conversazione', *Irish Naturalist*, v. 22, 1913, p. 16; 'A note on the Robertsonian Saxifrages', by R. Lloyd Praeger, *Irish Naturalist*, v. 21, 1912, pp. 205-6. ; E. Charles Nelson, *A Heritage of Beauty: The garden plants of Ireland, an illustrated encyclopaedia*, Dublin: Irish Garden Plant Society, 2000, p. 217.

12 *Irish Times*, 26 November 1907.

13 CFB, 'Verbascum Leiantham', *Gardeners' Chronicle*, 29 August 1908, p. 171.

14 CFB, 'Water Gardening', *Irish Gardening*, September 1907, pp. 167–8; CFB, 'Coleogyne Mooreana', *Irish Gardening*, February 1909, p. 25; CFB, 'Sophoras', *Irish Gardening*, August 1909, p. 117; CFB, 'Spiraea Ariaefolia', *Irish Gardening*, September 1909, p. 137.

15 Eileen McCracken, 'Nurseries and seed shops in Ireland', in Charles Nelson and Aidan Brady (eds), *Irish Gardening and Horticulture*, Dublin: Royal Horticultural Society of Ireland, 1979, pp. 184-7.

16 CFB, 'Current Topics', *Irish Gardening*, June 1910, p. 88.

17 G.N. Smith in *Gardeners' Chronicle*, 96: 43, 21 July 1934, quoted in E. Charles Nelson and Alan Grills, *Daisy Hill Nursery Newry: A history of the most interesting nursery probably in the world*, Belfast: Northern Ireland Heritage Gardens Committee, 1998, p. 106.

18 Kew MSS, DC 131, CFB to the Director, Kew Gardens, 18 September 1908; DC 131, CFB to the Director, 7 March 1913. Fred's letters to Kew were invariably signed either 'Yours truly' or 'Yours faithfully, C.F. Ball'.

19 Glasnevin MSS, D55/CB/2, W.J. Bean to CJB, 18 July 1913; 'Deutzia compacta', from the website Trees and Shrubs Online (treesandshrubsonline.org/articles/deutzia/deutzia-compacta/), accessed 14 August 2020.

20 RHS Lindley Library, E.A. Bowles Papers, 2.6.2.1., Moore to Bowles, 25 March 1907.

21 CFB, 'Irish Notes', *The Garden*, 28 August 1909; J.G.D. Lamb, 'Some Irish Horticulturists', in *Irish Gardening and Horticulture*, p. 94. Fred and Richard Beamish kept in touch and in May 1914 Fred sent him his *Calceolaria* cross (*Heritage of Beauty*, p. 33).

22 RHS Lindley Library, EAB/appendix/1.5.1, Moore to Bowles, 27 September 1907.

23 Lamb, 'Some Irish Horticulturists', p. 94, *A History of Gardening in Ireland*, pp. 142-7; see also *The Gumbleton Bequest*, online exhibition, National Botanic Gardens, Glasnevin, https://sway.office.com/qdBdJzzb2EiehP9T.

24 CFB, 'Irish Notes: Mr W. E. Gumbleton's Garden', *The Garden*, 2 October 1909, pp. 480-1; also, CFB, 'Olearias in Ireland', *Gardeners' Chronicle*, 28 January 1911, pp. 52-3; CFB, 'Meconopsis chelidonifolia, *Gardeners' Chronicle*, 11 April 1914, p. 248.

25 Glasnevin MSS, D55/CB/5, Gumbleton to CFB, 6 November 1910; *Brightest Jewel*, p. 210. Fred's comments which Gumbleton disputed were in 'Current Topics', *Irish Gardening*, November 1910, p. 163.

26 CFB to Alice, 3 December 1911.

Chapter 4: Botanizing in Europe

1 For the background, see J.W. Horsley, *I Remember: Memories of a 'sky pilot' in the prison and the slum*, London: Wells Gardner, Darton and Co, 1911, pp. 148–58, and Jack McInroy's informative account of the canon's interests and career: http://walworthsaintpeter.blogspot.com/2010/12/canon-horsley.html.

2 On Reginald A. Malby, see John Page, 'The Admirable Malby', *Quarterly Bulletin of the Alpine Garden Society*, Vol. 54, No. 1, March 1986, no. 223.

3 Reginald A. Malby, *With Camera and Rücksack in the Oberland and Valais*, London: Headley Brothers, n.d. [1913].

4 'S. Cotyledon in Nature', *Irish Gardening*, May 1914, pp. 72-3.

5   *With Camera and Rücksack in the Oberland and Valais*, pp. 56–7. Canon Horsley used photographs taken by both Fred and Malby for a lecture he delivered in January 1911 on 'The Scenery and People of the Bernese Oberland, including Swiss plants', illustrated by lantern slides ('Horticultural Club: Flora of the Bernese Oberland', *Gardeners' Chronicle*, 28 January 1912, p. 61). The arrival of a batch of 'Alpine plants' from 'C.J. Ball, Meirengen, Switz.', was recorded in the Glasnevin Donations Book (June 1909).

6   Fred told of the alligator at Mucklagh in a letter to Alice Kinghan, n.d. [1912]. I am grateful to Richard Page, a great-grandson of O'Mahony, for the information that the family still has the (now stuffed) alligator.

7   O'Mahony had already made a donation of some *Haberlea* from Bulgaria late in 1910, Glasnevin MSS, Accessions Register, November 1910.

8   C.F.Ball, 'Botanizing in Bulgaria', *Journal of the Royal Horticultural Society*, vol XXXIX, 1913, p. 2.

9   C.Q., 'The Rose Gardens of Europe', *The Garden*, 23 October 1915, p. 522. 'C.Q.' was Herbert Cowley's pseudonym. The address of O'Mahony's orphanage, recalling the statesman who was so admired in Bulgaria, was 23 Rue Gladstone, Sofia.

10 'Botanizing in Bulgaria', p. 2; CFB, 'Botanising in Bulgaria', *Gardeners' Chronicle*, 20 April 1912, p. 252; 'The Rose Gardens of Europe', p. 522. Cowley's jaundiced view of King Ferdinand would have been influenced by the King's recent decision (1915) to change sides in the First World War and join the Germans.

11 Fred wrote later that of the *Genista spathulata* he collected, only one plant survived the journey home but a couple of years it repaid the effort by producing 'a mass of bright yellow flowers' at Glasnevin, 'Some Bulgarian Novelties', *Irish Gardening*, July 1913.

12 'Botanising in Bulgaria', *Gardeners Chronicle*, 27 April 1912, p. 275; also, CFB, 'Haberlea rhodopensis', *Irish Gardening*, July 1914, p. 108.

13 A month later the Accessions register at Glasnevin recorded the arrival of 'A collection of Alpine Plants' from both Fred and 'His Majesty the King of Bulgaria'.

14 Kinghan Family Papers, CFB to Alice Lane, 22 July 1912.

15 Kew MSS, DC187, f. 282, CFB to Watson, 2 August 1912.

16 CFB, 'Primula Allionii', *Gardeners Chronicle*, 8 February 1913, p. 85.

17 CFB, 'A Search for Alpines in the Granite Region of the Maritime Alps', *Irish Gardening*, February 1914, pp. 28-9.

18 CFB, 'A Search for Alpines in the Granite Region of the Maritime Alps', *Irish Gardening*, March 1914, pp. 13-14. The Ciriega pass is known as Col de Cerise in French and Colle Ciriega in Italian.

19 CFB, 'Primula Allionii', *Gardeners' Chronicle*, 8 February 1913, p. 85.

Chapter 5: Editor of Irish Gardening

1 For background to Dublin's scientific community at this time, and the field club movement, see Seán Lysaght, *Robert Lloyd Praeger: The Life of a Naturalist*, Dublin: Four Courts Press, 1998, pp. 37-53.

2 'Dublin Naturalists' Field Club', *Irish Naturalist*, v. 17, 1908, p. 185.

3 'Dublin Naturalists' Field Club', *Freeman's Journal*, 19 October 1909, p. 4; 'Dublin Naturalists' Field Club', *Weekly Irish Times*, 23 Oct 1909, p. 2; DNFC archive, leaflet, 'Excursion to Powerscourt, Saturday, October 16th, 1909.

4 DNFC archive, minutes of committee meeting held at University College, 22 April 1910.

5 'Dublin Naturalists' Field Club, *Irish Naturalist*, v. 17, 1908, pp. 264-5; 'Dublin Naturalists' Field Club', *Irish Naturalist*, v. 19, 1910, p. 53; 'Dublin Naturalists' Field Club', *Irish Naturalist*, v. 20, 1911, pp. 71-2; DNFC archive, List of exhibits, 1908,1909 and 1910; *Reflections and Recollections: 100 years of the Dublin Natural-*

ists' Field Club, Dublin: Dublin Naturalists' Field Club, 1986, p. 21. Fred seems to have been a member of the committee of the DNFC from 1909 to 1912, probably stepping down during the course of 1912 as some committee members were required to do after serving a three-year term.

6   National Library of Ireland, MS 19,710-19,711, Minutes of Dublin Microscopical Club, minutes of meetings, 13 December 1911 and 11 December 1912.

7   'A note on the Robertsonian Saxifrages', by R. Lloyd Praeger, *Irish Naturalist*, v. 21, 1912, pp. 205-6.

8   Letter from Horace Plunkett, Department of Agriculture and Technical Instruction, Dublin, to the editor, *Irish Gardening*, 13 February 1906, in *Irish Gardening*, March 1906. Sir Horace Plunkett, a committed agricultural reformer, was so impressed with the plan for the new journal that he donated £10 towards its dissemination 'among likely readers, especially cottagers'. See also *Irish Gardening*, December 1908.

9   CFB to Alice, 20 November 1911.

10   CFB to Alice, 3 June 1913.

11   *Irish Gardening* 7, 1912, pp. 21-2.

12   Kew MSS, DC 187, f.282, CFB to William Watson, 2 August 1912.

13   C.B. Pike, 'Pruning for Apples', *Irish Gardening*, vol vii, no. 73, March 1912, pp. 36-7.

14   CFB to Alice, 22 July 1913; 'Trespass by sheep: four thousand apple trees injured', *Daily Express*, 25 February 1914, p. 2. Fred estimated the damage at £167 but the judge awarded Pike the sum of £75 after hearing that the defendants' expert witness estimate was £35.17s.6d.

15   CFB to Alice, 21 April 1913.

16   'Obituary', *Irish Gardening*, November 1915, p. 162.

17   'Obituary', p. 162.

Chapter 6: Alice

1   Kinghan Family Papers, CFB to Alice, 3 December 1911.

2   Quote from an undated draft letter from Alice [probably 1913] when applying for a job.

3   A letter from R.G. White, one of the trustees, to Alice, 8 January 1912, mentions her mother and suggests that 'bygones ought to be bygones' and that it was time to heal the rift between them.

4   CFB to Alice, n.d. [c. Sept 1913].

5   'Yes, there has been a very good show of chrysanthemums this year, at one time I used to think that you would get tired of flowers if you saw too much of them and consequently all connected with them would become an awful bore. Now I believe you're getting fonder of flowers, is that so?' (CFB to Alice, 1 October 1911).

6   CFB to Alice, 11 January 1912.

7   CFB to Alice, 20 November 1912.

8   CFB to Alice, 12 May [1912].

9   CFB to Alice, 22 July 1912. Herbert's death certificate cited 'phthisis' (tuberculosis) as the cause of his death.

10 CFB to Alice, n.d. [c. March 1912].

11 CFB to Alice, n.d. [c. March 1912].

12 CFB to Alice, 21 May 1913.

13 CFB to Alice, n.d. [1912].

14 CFB to Alice, n.d. [c. May 1912].

15 CFB to Alice, 5 June 1913. Fred wrote that he was pleased to hear Alice was going to get rooms with her mother as he thought this would be 'so much more pleasant for both of you', as long as 'you don't fight too much'.

16 CFB to Alice, 7 April 1913.

17 CFB to Alice, 19 March 1913.

18 Mary Ball to Alice, 20 March 1913.

19 CFB to Alice, 18 March 1913.

20 Constance Noar to Alice, 17 July 1913.

21 CFB to Alice, 14 April 1913.

22 CFB to Alice, 28 March 1913. This was Robert Strain (1845-1913), father of the better known master-builder and property developer, Alexander Strain (1877-1943).

23 CFB to Alice, 31 March 1913.

24 CFB to Alice, 3 June and 2 July 1913.

Chapter 7: Botanist of Gough Barracks, The Curragh

1 'Botanizing in Bulgaria', *Journal of the Royal Horticultural Society*, Vol XXXIX, 1913, pp. 1-11.

2 This began in 1910 and led to a highly critical letter being sent, Fred being among the signatories, about the way the affairs of Kew Guild were being conducted, and in particular the delays in the publication of the journal: *Kew Guild Journal*, 1909/10, p. 472.

3 Glasnevin MSS D55/CB/4, letters from W.R. Dykes; D55/CB/3 letters from E.A. Bowles.

4 Sheila Pim, *The Wood and the Trees: A Biography of Augustine Henry* (second edition), Kilkenny: Boethius Press, 1984, p. 169.

5 Kinghan Family Papers, CFB to Alice, 8 April 1913; Glasnevin MSS, D55/CB/6, letters from Augustine Henry; *Brightest Jewel*, pp. 220-23.

6 'E.B. Anderson, *Seven Gardens or Sixty Years of Gardening* (London: Michael Joseph, 1974), p. 24. See also George Sevastopulo, 'E.B. Anderson – the Dublin connection', Newsletter No. 47, winter 2007, Alpine Garden Society (Dublin Group), pp. 13-15. Anderson's memory is borne out by his frequent appearance in the Glasnevin donations book.

7 'Obituary', by F.W.M., *Irish Gardening*, vol X, no. 117, November 1915, p. 162.

8   'Plant notes: Globularia Incanescens', *Gardeners' Chronicle*, 25 July 1914, p. 69.

9   'New or noteworthy plants: Calceolaria × ballii', *Gardeners' Chronicle*, 14 February 1914, p. 102; *Heritage of Beauty*, p. 33.

10 'A hybrid Campanula', by J WB, *Irish Gardening*, August 1917, pp. 117–8; *Heritage of Beauty*, p. 38.

11 *Heritage of Beauty*, pp. 82–4; E.C. Nelson and Wendy F. Walsh, *An Irish Flower Garden Replanted*, Castlebourke: Edmund Burke, 1997, p. 161.

12 *Heritage of Beauty*, p. 82, quoting G. N. Smith in '*Escallonia C.F.Ball*', *Gardeners' Chronicle*, 96, 21 July 1934; *Daisy Hill Nursery*, p. 106; Glasnevin MSS, Donations Register, October 1920.

13 Henry Hanna, *The Pals at Suvla Bay: Being the record of 'D' Company of the 7th Royal Dublin Fusiliers*, Dublin: Ponsonby, 1917, p. 14.

14 Kinghan Family Papers, CFB to Alice, 6 November 1914.

15 CFB to Alice, 20 November 1914. I am indebted to Paul Nixon for the information, based on his analysis of service records, that Fred must have enlisted between 9 and 12 November (email to the author, 21 June 2021).

16 CFB to Alice, 24 November 1914.

17 'Obituary', by F.W.M., *Irish Gardening*, vol X, no. 117, November 1915, p. 162.

18 https://www.facebook.com/gallipoliassociation/posts/lance-corporal-eugene-duffy-2nd-battalion-royal-dublin-fusiliers/4903960116315258/ (accessed 12 January 2022). Duffy enlisted with the 1st battalion, Royal Dublin Fusiliers, but ended up in Gallipoli with the 7th. His poem, 'Gallipoli', is reproduced at the end of this book.

19 My thanks to Paul Nixon for this information, based on his analysis of service records (email to the author, 19 June 2021). Wilfred survived the war.

20 The story is retold in Turtle Bunbury, *The Glorious Madness: Tales of the Irish and the Great War*, Dublin: Gill and Macmillan, 2014, p. 201; Nelson and Walsh, *An Irish Flower Garden Replanted*, p. 161; Fionnuala Fallon in 'Garden of Tranquility', *Irish Times*, 16 August 2014 and 'Fallen Soldiers and white feathers', *Irish Times*, 27 August 2014. I am also indebted to Dr E.C. Nelson for his recollections of conversations with Major General Frederick Moore in the 1980s.

21 Kinghan Family Papers, CFB to Alice, n.d. [Nov 1914].

22 CFB to Alice, 24 November 1914.

23 CFB to Alice, 20 November 1914.

24 CFB to Alice, 24 November 1914.

25 I am most grateful to Matt Holmes, Glasnevin Heritage, for his assistance in identifying 'Melville' (No. 24 Ballymun Road) and its location: emails of 29 and 30 July 2020. The house stands to this day, the name 'Melville' just visible on the two front gate posts.

26 For the Gunning brothers, see https://www.dublincity.ie/library/blog/diary-gunning-brothers-company-d; https://northernbankwarmemorials.blogspot.com/2012/11/gunning-george-cecil.html.

27 *Pals at Suvla Bay*, p. 206; Frank M. Laird, *Personal Experiences of the Great War (an Unfinished Manuscript)*, Dublin: Eason & Son, 1925, pp. 3, 61. For Frank Laird's early life, see Carole Hope, *Frank Speaking: from Suvla to Schweidnitz*, H&K Publishing, 2021, pp. xxiv-xxvi. Laird was a graduate of Trinity College Dublin and in 1914 was employed as a first class clerk at the Metropolitan Police Court in Dublin.

28 *Pals at Suvla Bay*, pp. 238 and 244; Gunning Diary, 19 [81]. Sgt Sutcliffe took over as section leader in February 1915. Other members of No. 2 section I have identified are as follows: Guy Cranwill, Hugh Anderson, George Fisher, Connolly Norman, Douglas Philippe, John Guy.

29 *Personal Experiences of the Great War*, p. 15.

30 I am most grateful to David Power, South Dublin Libraries, and the staff of Clondalkin Library for their help in identifying the location of Flanagan's Quarry.

31 *Personal Experiences of the Great War*, pp. 15-16.

33 *Personal Experiences of the Great War*, pp. 14-15.

33 Quoted in *Pals at Suvla Bay*, p. 29.

Chapter 8: Gallipoli

1 Dublin City Library, Royal Dublin Fusiliers collection, Corporal Henry Kavanagh papers, Henry Kavanagh to Enock Kavanagh, 15 May 1915; *Personal Experiences of the Great War*, p. 19.

2 Gunning Diary, p. 7 [65].

3 Glasnevin MSS, Accession register, July 1915.

4 See http://www.early-photographers.org.uk/Leics%20M-O.html. and 1911 census.

5 Dublin City Library, Royal Dublin Fusiliers Association Archive, RDFA.018, Transcription of Douglas (Frank) and Cecil Gunning's Gallipoli Diary, p.4 [38]. Curiously, the Gunnings refer to Fred as 'John' Ball, though since they mention he was 'assistant keeper, Royal Botanic Gardens, Dublin' it is clearly Fred they are referring to. Page references are from the recent transcription of the typescript, itself typed from the handwritten original.

6 *Personal Experiences of the Great War*, p. 61.

7 Gunning Diary, p. 1 [32].

8 *Personal Experiences of the Great War*, p. 37.

9 'Extracts from letters of Mr C. F. Ball', *Irish Gardening*, vol X, no. 117, November 1915, p. 161.

10 Gunning Diary, p. 2 [33].

11 Gunning Diary, p.3 [34]; *Personal Experiences of the Great War*, p. 34. The Glasnevin cemetery was one of the largest and best

known cemeteries in Dublin.

12 *Personal Experiences of the Great War*, p. 37.

13 *Personal Experiences of the Great War*, pp. 39-40.

14 Gunning Diary, p. 4 [38]. Frank Laird recalled having seen Anderson 'in the middle of our first night at Suvla Bay, shot through the body, and in sore straights' (*Personal Experiences of the Great War*, p. 65).

15 *Pals at Suvla Bay*, p. 154; war medal record. Frank Laird and Hugh Anderson later ended up as fellow officers in the 8th (Service) Battalion, RDF, on the western front in France (*Personal Experiences of the Great War*, p. 105). I am also grateful to Roger Watts for his memories of Hugh Anderson, his grandfather.

16 *Personal Experiences of the Great War*, p. 47.

17 *Personal Experiences of the Great War*, p. 34.

18 Gunning Diary, p 9 [67].

19 Gunning Diary, pp. 14 [48] and 7 [65].

20 Myles Dungan, *Irish Voices from the Great War* (new edition), Dublin: Merrion, 2014, pp. 77-81.

21 A letter from Jeffreson saying he had had 'some very lucky escapes' was published in *The Irish Times* on 29 August, six days after his death: quoted in *Dublin's Great Wars*, p. 110.

22 Quoted in *Irish Voices from the Great War*, p. 90.

23 Glasnevin MSS, Accessions Book, August 1915.

24 Service record of William Lacey, courtesy Royal Irish Fusiliers Regimental Museum, Armagh; also, E. Charles Nelson, 'They gardened Glasnevin: A register of gardeners, labourers, student-apprentices and lady gardeners in the Botanic Garden at Glasnevin, Dublin 1795–1945', p. 26. Occasional Paper No. 4, available at http://botanicgardens.ie/wp-content/uploads/2018/02/They-gardened-Glasnevin-A-register-of-gardeners-labourers-student-apprentice-and-lady-gardeners-in-the-Botanic-Gardens.-pp.-66.pdf .

25 Gunning Diary, p. 9 [67].

26 War diary of the Assistant Director, Medical Services, 10th (Irish) Division, entry for 13 September 1915.

27 Letter from Paddy Tobin to his father, 13 August 1915, quoted in *Irish Voices from the Great War*, p. 70. Tobin was killed three days after this letter was written.

28 *Pals at Suvla Bay*, p. 127. The medical officer wounded was Lt. Cassidy, RAMC.

29 *Personal Experiences of the Great War*, p. 61.

30 Gunning Diary, p. 9 [67].

31 'In memoriam: Charles Frederick Ball', by J.W.B., *Kew Guild Journal*, 1916, p. 307.

32 See Commonwealth War Graves Commission, Lala Baba cemetery record: https://www.cwgc.org/find-records/ find-war-dead/casualty-details/606805/charles-freder- ick-ball/#&gid=1&pid=1. Philip Orr, *Field of Bones: An Irish division at Gallipoli*, Dublin: Lilliput Press, 2007, p. 237, asserts that Fred was buried at sea but this was not the case. His re- mains were transferred from his initial place of burial to the CWGC's new Lala Baba cemetery in 1923.

33 Richard S. Grayson, *Dublin's Great Wars: The First World War, the Easter Rising and the Irish Revolution*, Cambridge: Cambridge University Press, 2018, p. 109; *Pals at Suvla Bay*, p. 152.

34 Shortly after being transferred to Macedonia the 10th Irish Division, along with other allied forces, was forced to with- draw to northern Greece after being attacked by the Bulgarian army. In September 1917 the 10th Irish Division, including the 6th and 7th Dublins, was transferred to Egypt.

Chapter 9: Memories and Memorials

1 'In memoriam: Charles Frederick Ball', by J.W.B., *Kew Guild Journal*, 1916, pp. 307–8.

2 'Obituary: C. F. Ball', *The Garden*, 16 October 1915, p. 54.

3 'In memoriam: Charles Frederick Ball', pp. 307-8.

4   'Obituary', by F.W.M., *Irish Gardening*, vol X, no. 117, November 1915, pp. 161–2.

5   Kinghan Family Papers, J.W. de Hinch, Acting Hon. Secretary, Dublin Naturalists' Field Club, to Mrs Ball, 28 October 1915; F.W. Moore, Hon. Sec., Dublin Microscopical Club, to Mrs Ball, 16 October 1915.

6   Duffy was invalided back home from Gallipoli and rejoined the 2nd Battalion, Royal Dublin Fusiliers on the western front. He was killed in action on 26 December 1916, aged 32. His poem is from an unidentified newspaper cutting.

7   Nobody seemed to have noticed that his age on this headstone is incorrect. It gave his age as 36, but he actually died a month before his 36th birthday.

8   There is also an error on the St Mobhi's church memorial which has Fred as 'Fredrick' rather than 'Frederick'. Fred's name appears on two memorials in Loughborough. One is in the Grammar School, where 54 former members of the school lost their lives in the war; the other is in the Carillon Tower, erected in 1921 in the middle of the Queen's Park, Loughborough: see https://www.loughborough-rollofhonour.com/page6.htm#$HH2.

9   J.W.B., 'Obituary', *Kew Guild Journal*, 1916, p. 307; 'Alpine and Rock Plants', by JWB, *Irish Gardening*, April 1918, p. 60.

10   Irish Garden Plant Society, 'The ceremonial planting of Escallonia C.F. Ball at the Memorial Gardens', posted 29 June 2016, https://irishgardenplantsociety.com/the-ceremonial-planting-of-escallonia-c-f-ball-at-the-war-memorial-gardens, accessed 28 July 2020.

11   *Daisy Hill Nursery*, p. 39; 'An appreciation: the late Mr G. N. Smith', by Cdr F. Gilliland, title unknown but dated 25 March 1939 (courtesy Mr John Gilliland).

12   'Escallonia C. F. Ball', *Gardeners' Chronicle*, 21 July 1932, quoted in *Heritage of Beauty*, p. 83.

13   'Oak with unique history', *Londonderry Sentinel*, 10 April 1937. A shorter report, 'Acorn from Gallipoli', appeared in the *Belfast Newsletter* on the same date.

14 I am most grateful to John Gilliland, current owner of Brook Hall, for making this entry from his grandfather's journal available to me, and for supplying much background information. Seamus O'Brien, David Gilliland and Neil Porteous have also provided additional help and information on the Brook Hall 'Gallipoli oak'.

15 For the background to this, see Roderick Cameron, The Gallipoli Oaks Project, https://www.internationaloaksociety. org/content/gallipoli-oaks-project#:~:text=In%20May%20 2013%2C%20the%20National,Winter%2DCooke's%20acorns.

16 'Old Loughburian killed in the Dardanelles', *Loughborough Echo*, 8 October 1915. Alice's copy of *The Pals at Suvla Bay* (No. 68 of a run of 200) is inscribed 'Alice A. Ball, Melville, Glasnevin, 1917'.

17 Kinghan Family Papers, R.W. Kinghan to Alice, 23 July 1921.

18 Kinghan Family Papers, certificate from Philip Daly's 'Auto-mobile School and Chauffeurs Employment Bureau', 9 August 1918.

19 Kinghan Family Papers, Certificate of Discharge on Demo-bilization, 26 September 1919.

20 *Personal Experiences of the Great War*, p. 5.

21 Kinghan Family Papers, R.W. Kinghan to Alice, 24 November 1920. On Bloody Sunday, 21 November 1920, 12 British army officers were killed by the IRA. In retaliation British forces opened fire on civilians at a Gaelic football match at Croke Park, Dublin, killing 14 people and wounding many others.

22 Kinghan Family Papers, Robert Kinghan to Alice, 25 October 1921.

23 Kinghan Family Papers, Mary Ball to Alice Kinghan, 19 October 1932.

24 *Personal Experiences of the Great War*, p. 61.

25 Imperial War Museum, London, IWM ENI/1PHO/014/36, Mary Ball to Imperial War Museum, 3 August 1917, https:// www.iwm.org.uk/collections/item/object/1020012274.

Sources Consulted

Manuscripts and Archives

Gilliland archive, Brook Hall, Derry, N.I. (Frank Gilliland journal)

Imperial War Museum, London (Mary Ball letter, 1917)

Kinghan Family Papers

Loughborough Grammar School archives, Loughborough, Leics

National Archives Kew (War Diaries of 10th Division, 7th Battalion RDF, RAMC)

National Botanic Gardens, Glasnevin (Botanic Gardens and Dublin Naturalists' Field Club archive)

National Library of Ireland (Microscopical Club records in F.W. Moore papers)

RHS Lindley Library, London (E.A.Bowles papers)

Royal Botanic Gardens, Kew (Staff files, Director's correspondence files, William Dallimore 'Reminiscences')

Royal Dublin Fusiliers Association archive, Dublin City Library (Gunning Diary and Henry Kavanagh papers)

Royal Irish Fusiliers Regimental Museum, Armagh (Lacey service record)

Books and Articles

Anderson, E.B., *Seven Gardens or Sixty Years of Gardening*, London: Michael Joseph, 1974.

Bean, William, *The Royal Botanic Gardens, Kew: historical and descriptive*, London: Cassell, 1908.

Bunbury, Turtle, *The Glorious Madness: tales of the Irish and the Great War*, Dublin: Gill and Macmillan, 2014.

Catalogue of Peter Barr & Sons, autumn 1900.

Collins, Timothy, *Floreat Hibernia: A bio-bibliography of Robert Lloyd Praeger 1865-1953*, Dublin, Royal Dublin Society, 1985.

Daly, Mary E., *The First Department: A history of the Department of Agriculture*, Dublin: Institute of Public Administration, 2002.

Desmond, Ray, *Kew: The History of the Royal Botanic Gardens*, London: Harvill Press with Royal Botanic Gardens, Kew, 1995.

Desmond, Ray, and Hepper, F. Nigel, *A Century of Kew Plantsmen: A celebration of the Kew Guild*, Richmond: Kew Guild, 1993.

Dungan, Myles, *Irish Voices from the Great War* (new edition), Dublin: Merrion, 2014,.

Floud, Roderick, *An Economic History of the English Garden*, London: Allen Lane, 2019.

Grayson, Richard S., *Dublin's Great Wars: the First World War, the Easter Rising and the Irish Revolution*, Cambridge: Cambridge University Press, 2018.

Hanna, Henry, *The Pals at Suvla Bay: Being the record of 'D' Company of the 7th Royal Dublin Fusiliers*, Dublin: Ponsonby, 1917.

Hope, Carole, *Frank Speaking: From Suvla to Schweidnitz*, H&K Publishing, 2021.

Horsley, J.W., *I Remember: Memories of a 'sky pilot' in the prison and the slum*, London: Wells Gardner, Darton and Co, 1911.

Kildea, Jeff, *Anzacs and Ireland*, Cork: Cork University Press, 2007.

Laird, Frank M., *Personal Experiences of the Great War* (an Unfinished Manuscript), Dublin: Eason & Son, 1925.

Lamb, J.G.D. 'Some Irish Horticulturists', in Charles Nelson and Aidan Brady (eds), *Irish Gardening and Horticulture*, Dublin: Royal Horticultural Society of Ireland, 1979.

Lamb, Keith and Bowe, Patrick, *A History of Gardening in Ireland*, Dublin: National Botanic Gardens, 1995.

Lysaght, Seán, *Robert Lloyd Praeger: The Life of a Naturalist*, Dublin: Four Courts Press, 1998.

Malby, Reginald A., *With Camera and Rücksack in the Oberland and Valais*, London: Headley Brothers, n.d. [1913].

McCracken, Donal, *Gardens of Empire: Botanical institutions of the Victorian British Empire*, London: Leicester University Press, 1997.

McCracken, Eileen, 'Nurseries and seedshops in Ireland', in Charles Nelson and Aidan Brady (eds), *Irish Gardening and Horticulture*, Dublin: Royal Horticultural Society of Ireland, 1979.

Nelson, E. Charles, *A Heritage of Beauty: The garden plants of Ireland, an illustrated encyclopaedia*, Dublin: Irish Garden Plant Society, 2000.

Nelson, Charles and Brady, Aidan (eds), *Irish Gardening and Horticulture*, Dublin: Royal Horticultural Society of Ireland, 1979.

Nelson, E. Charles and McCracken, Eileen M., *The Brightest Jewel: A history of the National Botanic Gardens*, Glasnevin, Dublin, Kilkenny: Boethius Press, 1987.

Nelson, E. Charles, 'They gardened Glasnevin: A register of gardeners, labourers, student-apprentices and lady gardeners in the Botanic Garden at Glasnevin, Dublin 1795-1945'. Occasional Paper No. 4.

Nelson, E.C. and Wendy F. Walsh, *An Irish Flower Garden Replanted*, Castlebourke: Edmund Burke, 1997.

Nelson, E. Charles and Grills, Alan, *Daisy Hill Nursery Newry: A history of the most interesting nursery probably in the world*, Belfast: Northern Ireland Heritage Gardens Committee (1998).

Orr, Philip, *Field of Bones: An Irish division at Gallipoli*, Dublin: Lilliput Press, 2007.

Page, John, 'The Admirable Malby', *Quarterly Bulletin of the Alpine Garden Society* (A.G.S.), Vol. 54, No. 1, March 1986, no. 223.

Pim, Sheila, *The Wood and the Trees: A biography of Augustine Henry* (second edition), Kilkenny: Boethius Press, 1984.

Reflections and Recollections: 100 years of the Dublin Naturalists' Field Club, Dublin: Dublin Naturalists' Field Club, 1986.

Wallis, E.J. and Spooner, Herman, *The Royal Gardens at Kew Illustrated* (second edition, 1908).

Newspapers and Journals

Daily Express (Dublin)

Freeman's Journal

The Garden

Garden History

Gardeners' Chronicle

The Gardeners' Magazine

Irish Gardening

Irish Independent

Irish Naturalist

Irish Times

Journal of the Royal Horticultural Society

Kew Guild Journal

Londonderry Sentinel

Loughborough Echo

Quarterly Bulletin of the Alpine Garden Society

Sheffield Daily Telegraph

Weekly Irish Times

Index